HOW TO BUILD EVERYTHING YOU NEED

FOR YOUR BIRDS

From Aviaries................To Nestboxes

BY

DOMINIC LaROSA

ISBN: 1-4033-4686-0 (e-book)
ISBN: 1-4033-4687-9 (Paperback)
ISBN: 1-4033-4688-7 (Rocket Book)

Library of Congress Control Number: 2002092819

This book is printed on acid free paper.

Printed in the United States of America
Bloomington, IN

1stBooks – rev. 5/28/03

Table of Contents

INTRODUCTION v

THE AVIARY 1
    Portable, single flight
    Portable, single flight on glides
    Small, multi-flight
    The "A-Frame"
    The "Standard Composite"
        Optional Modifications to
        Layout, variations of
    All Weather, indoor-outdoor style 1
    All Weather, indoor-outdoor style 2
    Metal constructed

NEST BOXES 65
    Finches, small softbills
    Budgies, Lineonated Parakeets, Lovebirds, etc.
    Cockatiels, most Conures & similar
    Lorries, Lorikeets
    Larger Parakeets
    Large Parrot Types

MISCELLANEOUS EQUIPMENT 81
    Moisturizing Devices
    Feeding Equipment
    Hospital Quarters
    Shipping Container
    Carrying Case

WIRING YOUR AVIARY 99

Dominic LaRosa

INTRODUCTION

Many old-timers in the world of aviculture can recall their first feeble, though enthusiastic attempts to put together a simple wood and chicken-wire structure that was to represent ultimately a first proud "bird-flight." More often than not, the aftermath of that exhaustive first exercise proved to be an unsightly, sorry looking state of affairs. At best, the finished product proved operational enough, so far as providing reasonably adequate housing for his newly acquired feathered pets, but, at worst, it represented costs in time and money far in excess of what was originally intended and budgeted. The budding novice had indeed gotten off to a bad start!

The author has, himself, personally experienced these early tragedies —— only because there was simply little or no instructional material to be found anywhere on the subject! There were sporadic bits and pieces of information, to be sure, that one could pick from one or two available experts or out of avicultural publications, but they were usually sketchy at best, and often left the urgent questions unanswered and little for the imagination to work with. To some, this all must surely ring a familiar bell!

Sadly enough, there is still, today, a surprising lack of good, working information on this essential subject. Hence, the purpose of this book!

It is hoped that the reader who proposes to try his hand at constructing any of the designs contained in the following pages — be it the "Aviary Eleganti" or one of the simple Finch boxes — will experience the same personal enjoyment and pride in his endeavors as the author has experienced in preparing the basic guidelines for him.

The manual itself comprises several categories of avicultural equipment which might be considered the basic "essentials" required in the practice of good aviculture: housing, nesting, feeding and important miscellaneous equipment. Non-essential discussons have been purposely eliminated to keep the manual to the minimum size for the reader. The one-sided print format leaves room for the builders' own notes and design modifications, a format requested by many former bird club members and other readers.

The section on housing comprises the first, and, by far, the largest category. And rightly so, since it is usually the adequate and proper confining of his pets that is of utmost concern to the aviculturalist and, by virtue of the many variables to be considered in designing a dwelling-type structure, there is an abundance of material to be offered the reader.

A goodly amount of analysis and final proof-reading was expended to ensure that every drawing, diagram, chart and bit of technical data was presented as clear and concise as possible and that all additive figures and dimensions represented an absolute minimum of cumulative errors. Claiming no infallibility, however, the author wishes to express apologies in advance should, in fact, any dimensional contradiction or miscalculation be discovered.

Before embarking on any one of the projects presented here, it is suggested the reader take pains to carefully study the working drawing thoroughly, paying particular attention to the material callouts, sizes to be measured and cut, and quantities of identical pieces. These are areas of preparation where even slight mistakes can result in unnecessary added expense.

Dominic LaRosa

Whenever practical, the builder should keep to the lumber types specified. If, for various reasons, a substitute type is preferred, he should stay away from the redwoods. Aside from Redwood being a soft, and weak wood, the very substances it contains which make it remarkably resistant to decay, disease, and insects can be potentially detrimental to the health of birds, particularly the wood "chewers". The most common working woods, and the best for our purposes, are Pine and Douglas Fir. Clear Pine, although a beautiful wood and a pleasure to work with, is more expensive and, for our needs, is not necessary. All of the laminated woods specified in the material lists are of the exterior type plywood's which utilize water-proof glues in their manufacture.

Unless pieces of work are laid out accurately, it will be difficult to turn out a satisfactory job. Consistent use of a rule and a square in checking out all measurements as work progresses is a good habit to acquire and will help guarantee proper laying-out and perfect fitting of pieces. Lines and measurements should be marked with a very sharp pencil or metal point; never with a felt-tip pen or marker.

Power tools are not considered a prerequisite for building most of the projects described in this book, although the experienced craftsman or impatient beginner who has access to these tools will find them a great asset.

The only tools to consider essential for most of our needs are a hammer, hand saw, hand drill, an assortment of wood drill bits, several sizes of hole-saws that can be attached to the drill (for cutting nest box entrance holes), screw driver, medium-sized crescent wrench, pair of wire cutters, square, measuring tape and pencil.

Needless to say, the best tools will give the poorest service and results unless they are handled properly. The beginner might profit immensely by picking out one of the more simple projects to start with in order to test his ability to make precise measurements and use his tools correctly. This is particularly important where power tools are to be used for the first time.

As implied earlier, each one of the projects described has been designed and dimensioned according to the most popular notions among the professional breeders. Some ideas will be found to duplicate standard proven equipment of the types found in most pet shops and bird supply houses (at an expensive premium, incidentally). Other ideas stem directly from the personal experiences and considerable experimentation of the author in the raising and breeding of his own birds through the years.

By no means, however, should the reader feel confined to these ideas in totality simply because they are claimed "proven" or because they are widely accepted. In fact, many unique provisions are offered in many of the plans which do allow considerable deviations in size or form to be made at the discretion of the builder without materially affecting the basic design. One of the joys of aviculture, it must be remembered, comes from the ongoing experimentation and discovery of better, success-bearing methods and techniques of keeping birds in captivity so that they may fare as well or better in their artificially created environment — in terms of their health, happiness, and willingness to procreate — than they might in their native habitat. In his quest for these kinds of rewards, then, the hobbyist will want to deviate from set plans and implement the kinds of ideas he feels may be more conducive to the welfare of his particular birds. He is encouraged to do so.

Dominic LaRosa

Also left to the discretion of the builder is the mode and type of finish to be used on his completed project. An only precaution needing mention here is that any covering that is used on a surface which is accessible to a chewing bird should be of a lead-free, non-toxic formulation, which includes most paint brands found on the market today.

Weather-proofing for roofs and sidings of cages and flights should be considered in accordance with whatever the local climate dictates. For the milder climates, inexpensive aluminum-asphalt paints are available that apply to wood surfaces easily and provide sufficient protection against hot sun, moisture, and cool of the night and are particularly protective to externally used plywood's. More adverse climates will require additional covering in the form of asphalt saturated felts and roll-roofing's or, in extreme cases, slates or tiles. The reader, again, must use his own judgment here depending upon his particular local circumstances.

Dominic LaRosa

THE AVIARY

The beginner should condition his mind right at the outset that aviary construction need not be considered a matter of extreme technical complication but, rather, a simple exercise in discipline and patience coupled with his own desire to achieve a job well done. If he begins with this frame of mind, he is off to a good start.

PORTABLE, SINGLE-FLIGHT AVIARY

Figure 1 describes a simple, portable-type aviary that can be utilized for most of the smaller softbills, Finches and parrot-type birds, and is particularly suitable for raising and breeding parakeets where space is limited.

Note that normal servicing is done from the outside through a small, simply hinged trap door on the lower, left-hand corner of the back panel. The back panel itself is supported by hinging which will allow total entrance to the interior of the cage for any major servicing required.

Nests are externally mounted for easy inspection and tending of young and contain wire-mesh covers just under the hinged top to prevent accidental escapes. The concaved bottoms of the nest boxes help contain the eggs of parakeets and those other birds which normally do not use nesting materials. Instructions for achieving this concave are covered in the section on Nestboxes.

Frame construction is of standard 2" X 2" Pine or Douglas Fir lumber, as are the frames for most of the aviary designs. 2" X 2" lumber, incidentally, is found on the market to vary in actual size anywhere between 1-1/4" square to just under 2" square and, more often than not, averaging around 1-1/2" square! For sake of simple consistency, therefore, all framing is hereafter measured as 1-1/2" X 1-1/2" and any deviation from this lumber size purchased by the builder can and should be adjusted on the project plan he is working with.

After cutting each frame piece to size and before actually nailing one piece to another, drill undersized holes in the first piece so that it will accept nails without splitting. Use 8d or 10d (2-1/2 to 3 inches long) nails for all framing requirements, depending on the actual size (thickness) of the lumber purchased. A good rule for determining nail size is the nail should be long enough to go through one of the pieces of wood and a little more than half through the second piece. Use a least two nails at each union, as shown in the diagram.

Cut all panel pieces to size and nail in place as shown using, in this case, nails which are cement coated. The wire mesh should be cut from 1/2" mesh stock if the aviary is used, ultimately, for a variety of bird sizes, but, if it is to house primarily parakeets, lovebirds or larger birds, 1" stock should be sufficient, and less expensive. Staple or tack mesh in place.

The nest boxes shown are mostly suitable for budgies, parakeets and lovebirds but may be modified to suit other birds as well. Note, incidentally, that the roof of the aviary is dimensioned and attached so that there is ample overhang protecting the nest boxes from any inclement weather.

The roof should be finally covered with an aluminum-asphalt finish and, in extreme climates, additionally covered with asphalt-saturated felt or other good roofing. Additional exterior or interior finishing is optional.

Construction Notes & Sketch Pad

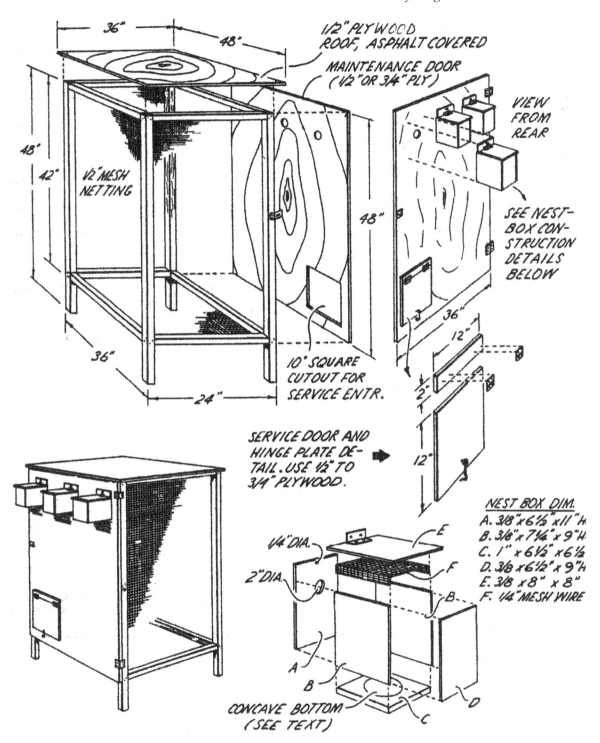

1/2" PLYWOOD ROOF, ASPHALT COVERED

MAINTENANCE DOOR (1/2" OR 3/4" PLY)

VIEW FROM REAR

36"

48"

48"

42"

1/2" MESH NETTING

36"

24"

48"

SEE NEST-BOX CON-STRUCTION DETAILS BELOW

36"

12"

2"

12"

10" SQUARE CUTOUT FOR SERVICE ENTR.

SERVICE DOOR AND HINGE PLATE DE-TAIL. USE 1/2" TO 3/4" PLYWOOD.

NEST BOX DIM.
A. 3/8" x 6½" x 11" h.
B. 3/8" x 7¼" x 9" h.
C. 1" x 6½" x 6½
D. 3/8" x 6½" x 9" h.
E. 3/8" x 8" x 8"
F. 1/4" MESH WIRE

1/4" DIA.

2" DIA.

E

F

B

A

B

D

C

CONCAVE BOTTOM (SEE TEXT)

FIGURE 1 – SIMPLE, PORTABLE TYPE AVIARY WITH CONVENIENT NORMAL & MAJOR SERVICE ACCESS. SUITED FOR MOST SMALLER SOFTBILLED BIRDS, FINCHES & PARROT TYPES.

3

Construction Notes & Sketch Pad

PORTABLE, SINGLE-FLIGHT AVIARY ON GLIDES

Figures 2 and 3 describe an aviary which offers a unique combination of two, seemingly incompatible advantages; it is large and roomy in size, spreading over three feet wide by six feet long by four feet high, yet it is highly portable (via an arrangement of built-in slides at its' base) and very ideal in situations where a more permanently fixed structure is not desired for various reasons. There is a generous amount of closed-in area for the protection of its' inhabitants against the elements, and a sufficient amount of open-air space is provided as well.

Normal and major servicing of the flight is done from the rear of the flight, as is the case with the nestboxes which are externally mounted on the rear panel.

Construction details, material requirements and additional data for this aviary are given in Figure 3 and should require no further elaboration here.

Construction Notes & Sketch Pad

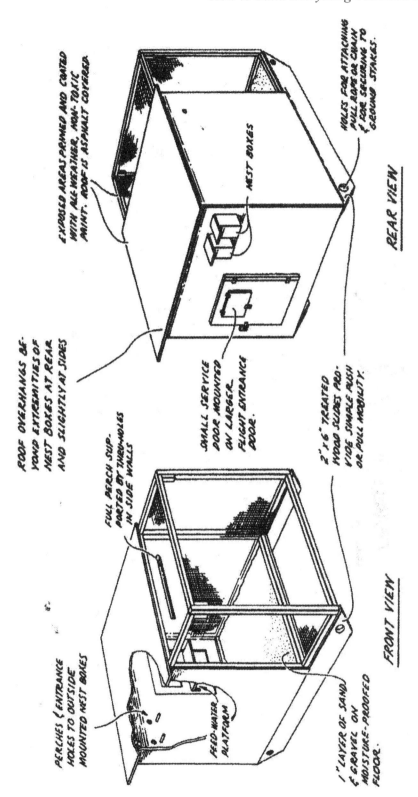

FIGURE 2 – MOBILE AVIARY ON SLIDES. DESPITE THE GENEROUS SIZE AND APPARENT WEIGHT OF THIS AVIARY, IT HAS A PRIME ADVANTAGE OF BEING EASILY MOVABLE BY MEANS OF BUILT-IN SLIDES ON ITS BASE. SUITABLE FOR A VARIETY OF SOFTBILLS, FINCHES & LOVEBIRD TYPES.

Construction Notes & Sketch Pad

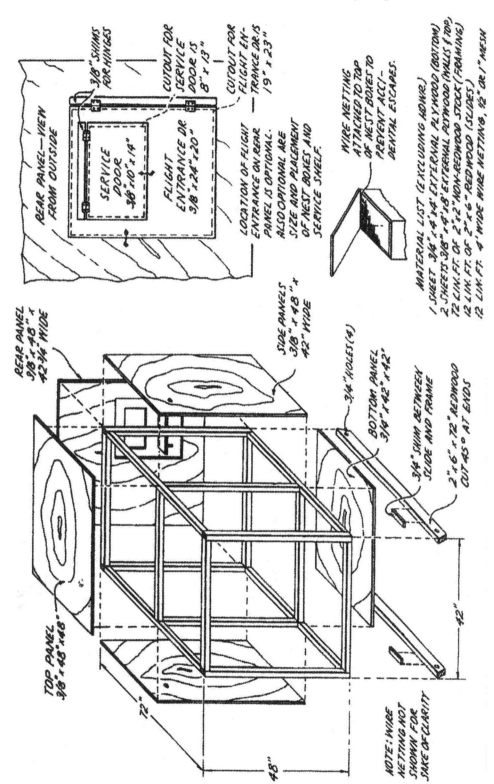

FIGURE 3 – MATERIAL LIST AND CONSTRUCTION DETAILS OF THE MOBILE AVIARY ON SLIDES.

Dominic LaRosa

Construction Notes & Sketch Pad

SMALL, MULTI-FLIGHT AVIARY

Figure 4 is a uniquely styled aviary in that, although it is impressive to the eye and literally generous in interior area, it is really quite small in perimeter. In this respect, it is an ideal structure for the aviculturist who has only restricted land area available for his hobby.

Also unique in design of this aviary is its modular construction concept. At the option of the builder, fewer or more individual flights can be planned for construction right at the outset, or deleted or added later as his needs dictate, without materially affecting the basic plan of the structure.

Construction is really not as difficult as it might at first appear. Two basic panel-types are prefabricated in quantity and serve as the initial, basic framework for the aviary. These are the "flight-front" panel (**A**) and the "flight-side" panel (**B**) as shown in the diagram.

After constructing the required number of the above panels per instructions, construction of the actual aviary begins with the laying out and nailing together (or bolting, if preferred) all the panels required for one row of flights first. At this point, the framework will stand unsupported and must be leveled accurately and "squared-up" in preparation for the rear panels (**E**), The rear panels are next attached, using cement coated nails, and the total structure again checked for squareness. The roof panels (**D**) are then, finally, attached.

Before proceeding with the opposite row of flights, fabricate and join the aviary entrance panel (**C**) to the forward flight-side panel (**B**) as shown in the illustration. An identical panel (**C**) is fabricated, with or without the door portion, and joined to the flight side panel at the far end. These panels now dictate the spacing (distance) between both rows of flights or, said differently, will ultimately provide for a three foot wide safety-passage (escape trap) for the aviary, as well as a convenient service passage.

Proceed with the second row of flights, following the same steps, but adding this time the support blocks as shown in the top center illustration of Figure 4 (note, also, detailed illustration at left center). After the framing and roofing is completed, attach 1/2 inch or 1 inch mesh wire netting throughout, as shown, preferably stapling from the interior sides of the flights so as to give added protection to the exposed frame parts against chewing type birds. Most builders, including the author, prefer to attach the netting during the prefabrication phase, just after the initial panels are individually fabricated and before they are attached together. The wire is much easier to work with at this stage, the finished panels are much sturdier and will not succumb to rougher handling during the installation stages.

An exterior, protective finish should finally be applied to all externally exposed surfaces, and appropriate weather protection applied to the roof.

An additional word about protection: in areas where soil tends to retain an excessive amount of moisture or where wood-rot or other similar damages are known to be common occurrences, particularly with wood structures that rest directly on the earth, it would be wise to treat all base portions of the framing with a good waterseal preparation sold on the market for this purpose before assembling in place. An even better method of coping with these potential rot problems is to set the entire framework structure on concrete blocks or cement foundation. Again, the method used will be left to the discretion of the builder who is familiar with his particular local situation.

<u>Construction Notes & Sketch Pad</u>

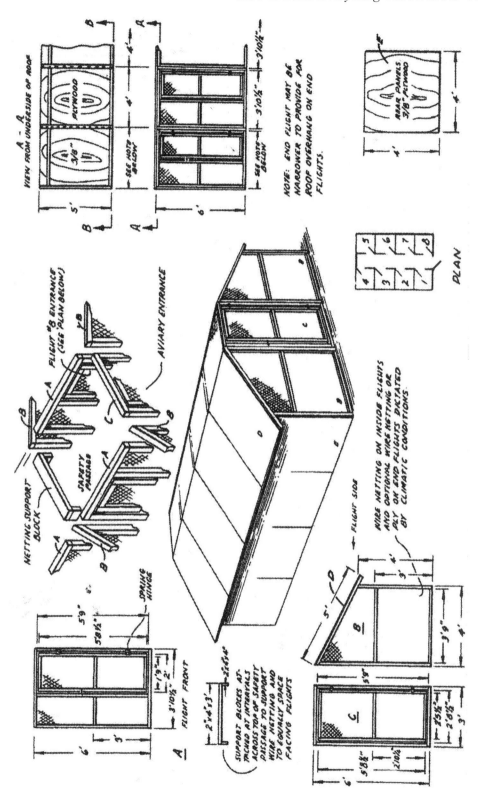

FIGURE 4 – THOUGH IMPRESSIVE IN APPEARANCE, ACTUAL SIZE OF THIS AVIARY (AS PICTURED WITH 8 FLIGHTS) IS ONLY 11' WIDE BY 16' LONG BY 6' HIGH AT THE CENTER. SUITABLE FOR THE SMALLER BIRDS, IT IS ALSO IDEAL TRANSIENT QUARTERS FOR YOUNG, OUT-OF-NEST BIRDS.

Construction Notes & Sketch Pad

THE A-FRAME AVIARY

Figure 5 describes a spacious aviary which employs the triangle concept in its' basic design and, as such, would be difficult to match, in terms of solid strength and sturdiness. Cockatiels and other small-to-medium sized birds seem more content in this pleasing, angled habitat with its' high-up, out of view seclusion (which offers ideal breeding privacy), and its' open-aired, free-flight area which is more than ample for all the exercise needed.

The optional safety passage provides worry-free entrance to the flight interior where servicing and maintenance chores may be accomplished with standing room ease.

Construction is relatively not difficult, in view of the very minimal amount of measuring that is required. The only difficulty that may be encountered, in fact, is in cutting the angles at the ends of each roof beam, twenty-eight angle cuts in all!

Assembly begins with the laying out of standard, hollow construction blocks on a 12 foot square perimeter (and mortaring same together, if desired). At 3 or 4 foot intervals, cement is poured into the hollows, after which the pre-cut, 2" X 6" wood bases are set in place as shown, and 50d (5-1/2") nails are driven through the fresh cement. When set, this arrangement will prevent any lateral movement of the framework. An even better method is to use 6" or longer foundation bolts to tie down the bases. The bolts are first set into the fresh cement, leaving at least 3" exposed above the top of the block, over which the bases (pre-drilled with oversized holes to readily accept the bolts) are placed. When the cement has hardened, the bases are then secured tightly by means of washers and nuts.

The two ten-foot uprights and top ridge are next pre-cut, assembled, and held in position with temporary scrap-wood braces, while the rafters (referred to above as roof-beams) are attached. The rafters are placed at two-foot spaced intervals, measured and marked along the base-plates and the ridge. Before the temporary braces are removed, the plywood roofing is attached and secured in place with cement coated nails. Provided the two foot spacing of the rafters has been measure correctly, the vertical edges of the roofing with set directly on the rafters for nailing purposes. However, the builder may prefer to measure and attach the furthermost pair of rafters somewhere within the two foot distance and so provide for a protective roof overhang (the diagram will have to be studied to understand this suggestion).

All open areas are next wire-netted with 1/2" or 1" wire mesh, depending on the sizes of the birds to be housed. The rear end of the structure may be wire-netted as well or, where more secure protection against the elements is desired, it should be covered with 1/2" exterior plywood.

The safety passage at the rear is an optional feature. A simple, 3-foot square, wire-netted structure, 6 foot high with a simply-framed entrance door, or even a canvas curtain, will suffice nicely.

Nesting boxes, both size and placement, are likewise optional, and again depend on the proposed inventory of bird sizes.

Final finishing and protective roof covering of all exposed wood surfaces should be dictated by local climatic conditions.

Construction Notes & Sketch Pad

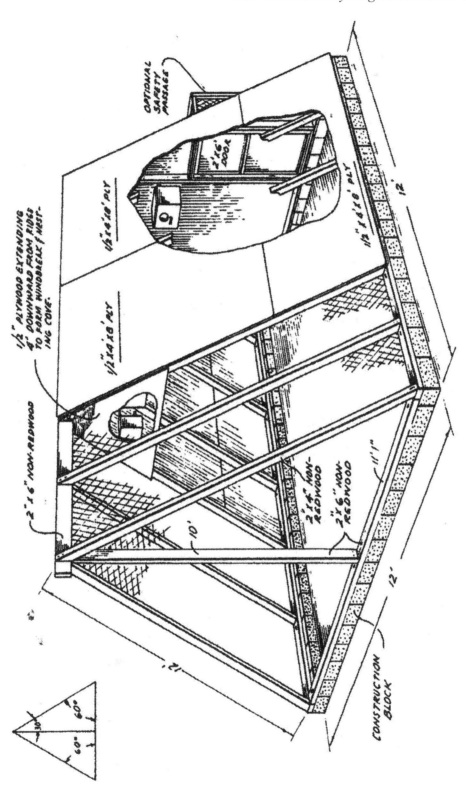

FIGURE 5 – THE A-FRAME. SUITABLE FOR COCKATIELS AND MEDIUM-SIZE, PARROT-TYPE BIRDS – OR A MIXED VARIETY – THIS AVIARY OFFERS VISIBLE SPACIOUSNESS, DURABILITY, PLEASING & NATURAL APPEARANCE, EASE OF MAINTENANCE AND IS EASY TO BUILD. THE CONCRETE BLOCK FOOTING PROVIDES SOLID, DAMAGE-PROOF AND LONG-LASTING ANCHORAGE OF THE FRAME.

17

Construction Notes & Sketch Pad

THE "STANDARD COMPOSITE" AVIARY

Figures 6 through 15 begin to test the builders' skill. This is a truly beautiful structure, both esthetically and operationally, and has all the features one could desire in an aviary, save the luxury of electrical and plumbing facilities. Yet, it is remarkably economical and relatively easy to put together, once the builder studies and fully understands the construction details.

Essentially, the design of this aviary is a somewhat sophisticated extension of the previously described "Modular Concept" where the completed form of a designed structure is equal to the sum of its' completely identical parts. The total structure may be expanded or reduced in useful area simply by adding or subtracting any number of identically prefabricated building blocks, or, in our case, "standard flight units", without materially affecting the continual versatility of the basic design. The aviary may "grow" or "diminish" in size, according the interests of the hobbiest.

The flight unit is, itself, composed of a number of identically fabricated building blocks. These blocks, hereafter referred to as "panels", are unique in that, although they are each assigned specific roles as integral parts of the total flight, the individual wood pieces that go to make them up are basically dimensioned, cut to size, and fabricated identically! It may be too premature to expect the reader to grasp the full implications of this, but they will become apparent as we go on.

Figure 6, The first illustration of the series, depicts the finished aviary, along with several hints of landscaping possibilities that lend themselves very nicely to the architecture. In the upper right-hand corner of the drawing are two interior plans which are suggested to the builder, either of which will retain the basic exterior design. Plan A offers the builder 9 individual flights measuring 4 feet wide by 8 feet long by 6 feet high each, and set in two facing rows which are separated by a 4 foot wide and 20 foot long, convenient passageway. The passage way, utilized as a service area and escape trap, leads, at its' center, into another 4 X 8 room which is used as a storage compartment and extended escape trap, and through which entrance is made to the aviary from the outside. The total plan nicely accommodates those softbills and parrot-type birds which are medium to small in size.

Plan B offers 5 flights suitable for the above birds, but converts the 4 remaining flights into two, 20 foot long compartments, providing extended flight area that is more than adequate for the needs of the larger type birds. **Figure 15** illustrates a third plan (note the drawing, 13th from the top) which may be even more compatible with the builders' requirements.

In any event, each of the above plans comprise the same basic elements in construction.

Construction Notes & Sketch Pad

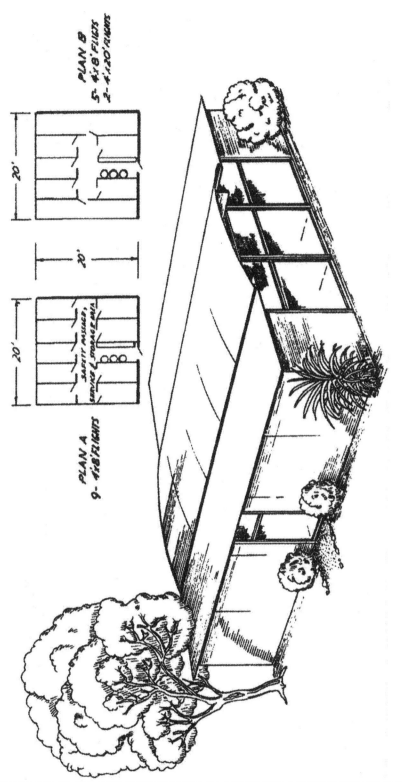

FIGURE 6 – A PLEASURE TO CONSTRUCT FROM THE STANDPOINTS OF BOTH BEAUTY AND ECONOMICS, THE ABOVE ENCLOSURE WAS PUT TOGETHER FROM STANDARD TYPE, PRE-FABRICATED UNITS (FLIGHTS) BOLTED TOGETHER AND CENTRALLY COVERED & WEATHER-PROTECTED ABOVE WITH A BEAUTIFULLY CURVATURED ROOF OF TRANSLUCENT FIBERGLASS.

21

<u>*Construction Notes & Sketch Pad*</u>

Figure 7 The basic panel, illustrated and detailed in this drawing is a 46-1/2 inch wide by 72 inch high affair which serves as the standard perimeter to be used for all the major panel-types. There are five of these major types: as show, they are the front-panel, forward-side-panel, rear-side-panel, rear-panel, and roof-panel. Two additional smaller types—the forward-top-panel and the door-panel—are likewise both constructed identically.

For sake of clarity, all the panels are assigned a code number corresponding though their individual functions and assembly-place on the completed flight. The lower right-hand figure in Figure 7 describes the coding system.

Note that all seven panel-types contain wood-pieces that are cut to 43-1/2 inches long. Note, also, that the two minor panel-types, the panels referred to in Figure 7 as #5 and #1a, contain pieces cut to 24 inches long. In other words, only three basic framing measurements are required for all the paneling that is needed to construct one or any number of flights! As such, lumber can be purchased pre-cut, and all framing constructed almost production-line style—representing both as saving in lumber costs and in construction time! Indeed, the builder will appreciate the simplicity of the actual fabrication, as well, as we progress!

A unique little device is essentially responsible for the design feature that makes it possible to build so large a structure with so few, differently measured cuts of material. This little device is what is referred to, hereafter, as a "spacer." It is not absolutely necessary that the reader understand the full ramifications of the role played by the "spacer", but close analysis of the construction diagrams and illustrations will reveal how, without this device, each panel type would have to be measured independently different than its' neighboring panel, if proper fit was to be guaranteed. And, in addition to the excessive costs in time and money that would result, all the versatility of the initial design would disappear. There could be only one layout plan with no provisions for inter-changeability of panel types in order to expand, reduce, or adjust total flight area to suit.

And so the necessity of the "spacer," which is simply a length of 2" X 2" board used for filling up the corner spaces left when two or more standard flight units are joined together, each flight sharing a side wall with its' adjacent neighboring flight. Detailed application of the spacer is more fully illustrated in Figures 9, 10 and 11.

Figure 8 presents a greatly detailed, working chart which will assist the builder in computing material quantities and costs involved in the total aviary project. Additional information has been included should it be preferred to construct an expanded or lesser version of the aviary as it is depicted in Figure 6.

The first column in the chart indicates the total number of flight-units the builder proposes to construct in a single row. Opposite that number, in adjacent columns, he is given the quantities of the various-sized wood-pieces required to fabricate that number of flight-units. He is additionally given the quantity of wire-netting he must purchase as well as the total square feet of exposed wood surfaces that will require painting. The chart is invaluable as a time saver and will spare many errors in judgment and accompanying headaches usually experienced in trying to compute larger projects such as this one.

Construction Notes & Sketch Pad

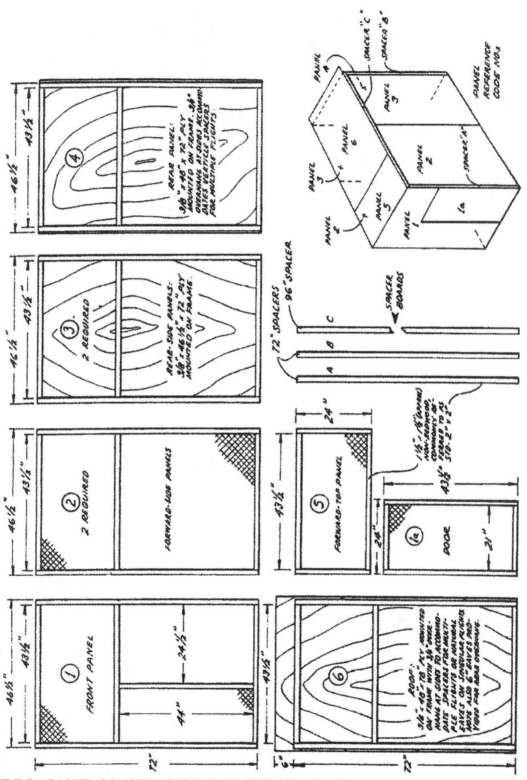

FIGURE 7 – PANEL CONSTRUCTION FOR THE STANDARD COMPOSITE FLIGHT-UNIT, A 4'X8'X6' HIGH FLIGHT. THE UNIQUE EMPLOYMENT OF "SPACER" BOARDS IN THE ULTIMATE ASSEMBLY OF THE AVIARY ALLOWS ALL MAJOR FRAMING OF THE DIFFERENT PANELING TO BE PRE-FABRICATED IDENTICALLY. REFER TO FIGURE 8 FOR CUTTING REQUIREMENTS.

<u>**Construction Notes & Sketch Pad**</u>

# OF FLIGHTS	# OF INDIV PANELS REQ'D (PANEL NUMBER)						# OF REQ'D SPACERS			# OF 2'X2' LENGTHS TO CUT						3/8" PLYWOOD REQUIRED			48" WIDE NETTING (LINEAR FEET)			PAINT REQ'D (***) SQ.FT
	#1	#2	#3	#4	#5	#6	36" "A"	72" "B"	96" "C"	96"	72"	44"	43-1/2"	24"	21"	(PANEL #3) 46-1/2"X6'	(PANEL #4) 4'X6'	(PANEL #6) 4'X6-1/2'	REQ'D (*)	FLOOR (**)	TOTAL	
1	1	2	2	1	1	1	0	0	0	0	14	1	25	2	2	2	1	1	20	8	28	280
2	2	3	3	2	2	2	1	1	1	1	26	2	44	4	4	3	2	2	34	16	50	490
3	3	4	4	3	3	3	2	2	2	2	38	3	63	6	6	4	3	3	48	24	72	700
4	4	5	5	4	4	4	3	3	3	3	50	4	82	8	8	5	4	4	62	32	94	910
5	5	6	6	5	5	5	4	4	4	4	62	5	101	10	10	6	5	5	76	40	116	1120
6	6	7	7	6	6	6	5	5	5	5	74	6	120	12	12	7	6	6	90	48	138	1330
7	7	8	8	7	7	7	6	6	6	6	86	7	139	14	14	8	7	7	104	56	160	1540
8	8	9	9	8	8	8	7	7	7	7	98	8	158	16	16	9	8	8	118	64	182	1750
9	9	10	10	9	9	9	8	8	8	8	110	9	177	18	18	10	9	9	132	72	204	1960

(* - PANELS #1, #1a, #2, #5)
(** - FLOOR IS OPTIONAL)
(*** - AMOUNTS GIVEN FOR PAINT ARE APPROXIMATE ONLY AND REPRESENT SQUARE FEET OF EXPOSED SURFACES)

FIGURE 8 – MATERIAL QUANTITIES REQUIRED FOR ANY DESIRED NUMBER OF FLIGHTS IN THE STANDARD AVIARY. THE "# OF FLIGHTS" COLUMN REPRESENTS THOSE NUMBERS OF FLIGHTS WHICH THE READER PROPOSES TO DESIGN IN A SINGLE-ROW FASHION. IT WILL BE NOTED THAT EACH WALL IS COMMON TO ITS ADJOINING FLIGHT, WITH THE EXCEPTION, OF COURSE, OF THE END FLIGHTS. WHERE TWO OR MORE ROWS OF MULTIPLE FLIGHT SYSTEMS ARE PROPOSED, THEREFORE, IT IS NECESSARY TO CALCULATE THE MATERIAL

Construction Notes & Sketch Pad

Figure 9 shows an "exploded" view of the single flight-unit, illustrating how the individual panel-types are fitted together. Note again the positions and functions of the spacers (labeled A, B and C).

All paneling is bolted together using 1/4" bolts and nuts. Approximate placement of the holes drilled for this purpose is also shown in the illustration (Figure 9). It is suggested that, before initially fabricating the pre-cut lumber into panels, a jig device be set up on a drill press, or if a hand-drill is used, a wood or cardboard pattern of a sort be made which can automatically and accurately measure off the correct hole locations, all wood-pieces should be pre-drilled while they are still easy to handle.

Although the nut-and-bolt method of fastening flight panels together is preferred, since it allows for easier readjustment of flight or floor plan at later dates, the use of nails is not discouraged.

Figure 10 shows details for the use of spacers mentioned above.

Figure 11 shows the aviary taking form with one row of flights nearing completion. At this point, the assembled units are essentially operational and may be put into use while the remaining construction work continues.

In the illustrations, note the 2" X 6" baseplate which supports the total perimeter of each flight at its' footing. It is essential that the boards be chemically treated (with an appropriate moisture and vermin-proofing preparation sold on the market) before being placed in this position in direct contact with the soil. In extreme soil and climate conditions, and where a more solid footing is desired, the builder may want to consider using concrete or construction blocks for this purpose, as described in the preceding section on the "**A-Frame Aviary**" and its' subsequent sections.

Before construction is begun on the second row of flight-units of the aviary, an additional panel #2 (forward-side-panel) is attached adjacent to the outer side of the last flight of the completed rows so that it encloses that end of what eventually is to become the center passageway of the aviary. One more such panel is attached in similar fashion to the outer side of the first flight. The two panels not only serve to "close up" the ends of the eventual passageway but also dictate the spacing, or distance, between the two rows of flights. Additionally, the panels provide overhead support for the wire-netting which is eventually strung across the top of the passageway. The passageway will, in fact, become entirely enclosed, except for the entranceway into the storage area, which, itself, will be closed-in from the outside work, thus providing a large, somewhat sophisticated trap for birds who escape their flight. The wire-netting, incidentally, is applied over the passageway, straddling the top, inboard edges of both flight rows. Additional support may be provided for the weight of the netting by installing extra #2 panel frames (with their innards removed) at intervals along the passageway. These will also help give support to the overhead cross-beams which are installed before applying the fiberglass roofing, all of which will be explained later.

The exposed plywood roofing is next sealed and weatherproofed, the choice of materials left to the builders' option.

<u>Construction Notes & Sketch Pad</u>

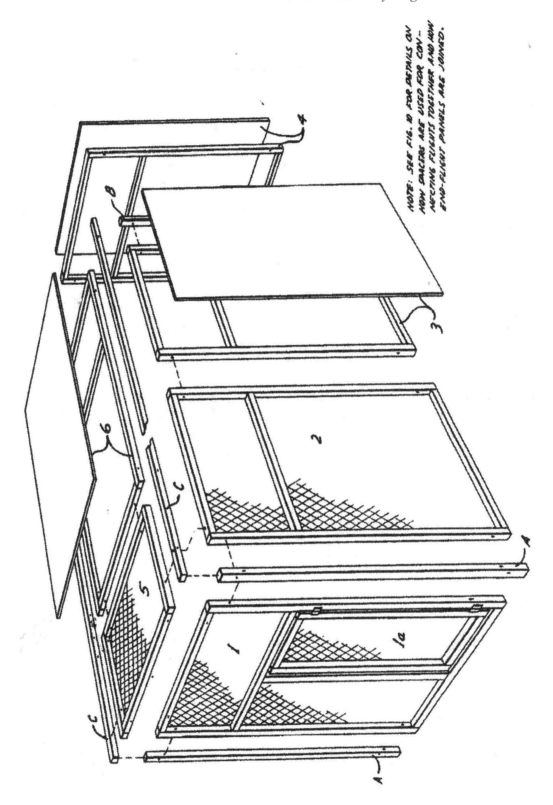

NOTE: SEE FIG. 10 FOR DETAILS ON HOW SPACERS ARE USED FOR CON- NECTING FLIGHTS TOGETHER AND HOW END-FLIGHT PANELS ARE JOINED.

FIGURE 9 – EXPLOSION VIEW SHOWING HOW ALL PANELS DETAILED IN FIGURE 7 (Pg. 24) ARE JOINED TOGETHER TO FORM ONE OF THE "FLIGHT UNITS" OF THE STANDARD-COMPOSITE AVIARY. FARSIDE PANELS DELETED FOR CLARITY.

Dominic LaRosa

<u>*Construction Notes & Sketch Pad*</u>

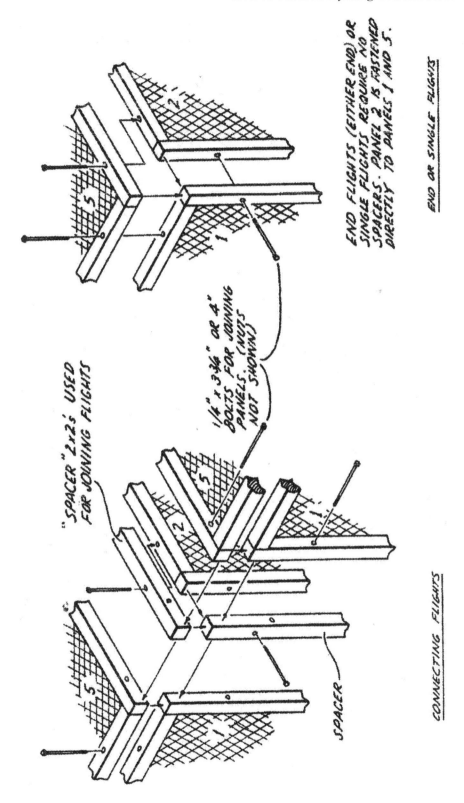

FIGURE 10 – THE USE OF "SPACERS" IN THE JOINING TOGETHER OF FLIGHTS IN THE STANDARD COMPOSITE AVIARY. THE END FLIGHTS REQUIRE NO SPACERS.

Construction Notes & Sketch Pad

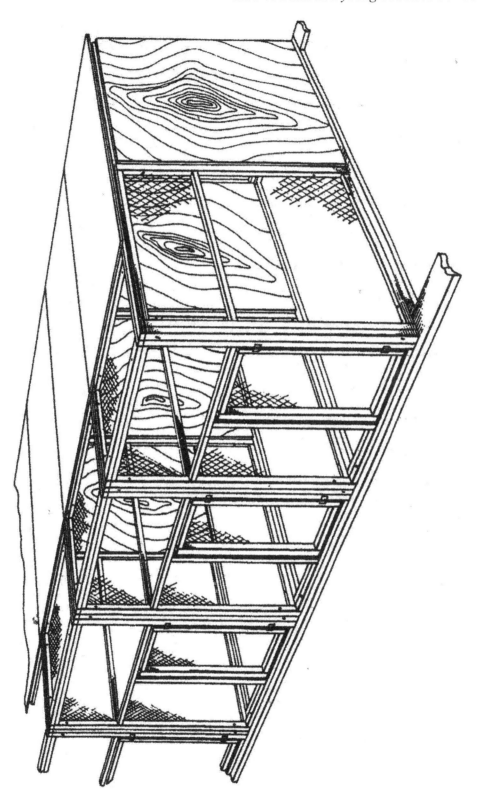

FIGURE 11 – THE COMPOSITE AVIARY TAKING SHAPE WITH THE FIRST ROW OF FLIGHTS NEARING COMPLETION.

Construction Notes & Sketch Pad

Figure 12 Finally, the fiberglass cover is applied as shown. Although a good number of translucent color-shades are available on the market which allow a pleasing display of sunlight to come through, the white, or off-white, transparent colors seem to allow the most beneficial rays to penetrate and, as such, are the preferred colors for our purposes.

2" X 2"s are placed 9 feet apart on the roof of the aviary, parallel to the length of the passageway and nailed through the plywood roofing and into the framing material underneath. The boards, both 21 feet long, will be found to overlap the ends of the passageway by about 6 inches at each end. Another single board, 2" X 6" X 21 feet long is then located and fastened on its' edge directly parallel to and down the center of the passageway roof. The resulting distance between the center board and the two outer boards should measure approximately 4-1/2 feet. The glass panels are next installed at right-angles to the boards, overlapping each panel with the next as they are fastened directly to the three boards, using galvanized and washered nails for the fastening.

Painting and miscellaneous finishing of exposed wood parts are left to the personal tastes of the builder.

The service and storage room should be arranged with convenient shelving and storage bins that will facilitate the hobbyists' needs.

An appropriate gravel may be spread throughout the floor area, after which proper perching, feeding, and watering equipment is installed and the aviary is considered operational.

Figure 13 suggests several optional modifications that the builder may choose to employ for his needs in building the aviary.

Figures 14 and 15 illustrate additional ideas for aviary layouts using the basic flight-unit described in this section.

Dominic LaRosa

<u>*Construction Notes & Sketch Pad*</u>

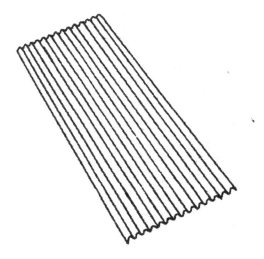

TRANSLUCENT FIBRE-GLASS SHEETS, AVAILABLE IN 26" WIDTHS (2" USED IN OVERLAPPING ADJACENT PIECES). TEN-10-FOOT LONG PIECES ARE REQUIRED.

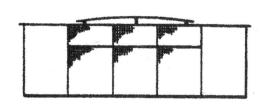

PLAN SHOWING EDGE VIEW OF CURVED FIBRE-GLASS ROOF STRADDLING 2"x6" BEAM AT CENTER AND 2"x2½" AT EDGES.

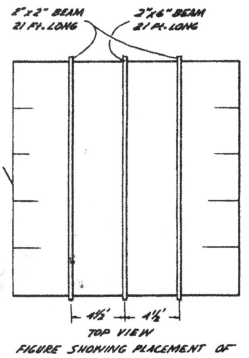

2"x2" BEAM 21 FT. LONG

2"x6" BEAM 21 FT. LONG

4½' — 4½'

TOP VIEW
FIGURE SHOWING PLACEMENT OF BEAMS USED FOR SUPPORTING FIBRE-GLASS

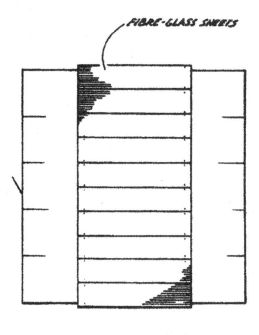

FIBRE-GLASS SHEETS

TOP VIEW
FIBRE GLASS PANELS INSTALLED & NAILED TO BEAMS. USE FELT NAIL-WASHERS

FIGURE 12 – DETAILS DESCRIBING INSTALLATION OF THE CORRUGATED FIBERGLASS PORTION OF THE COMPOSITE-AVIARY ROOFING.

Construction Notes & Sketch Pad

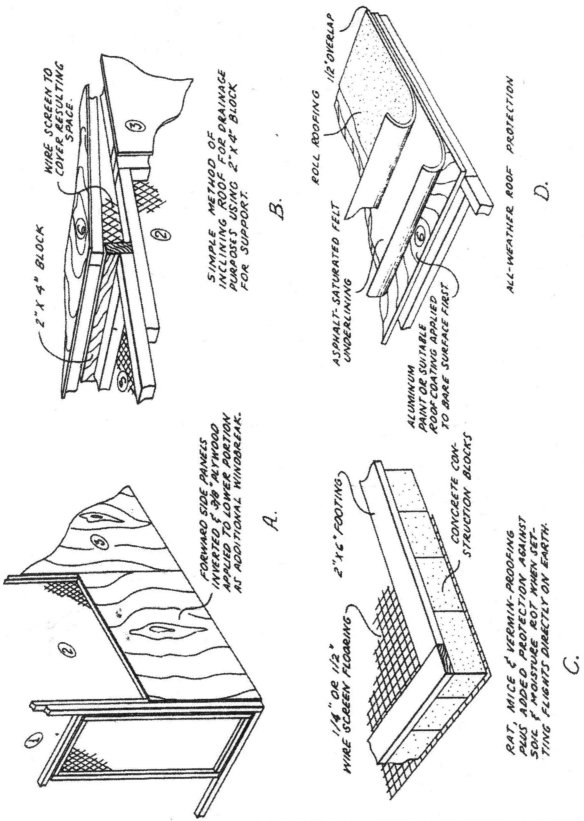

FIGURE 13 – OPTIONAL MODIFICATIONS SUGGESTED IN THE CONSTRUCTION OF THE COMPOSITE AVIARY.

<u>*Construction Notes & Sketch Pad*</u>

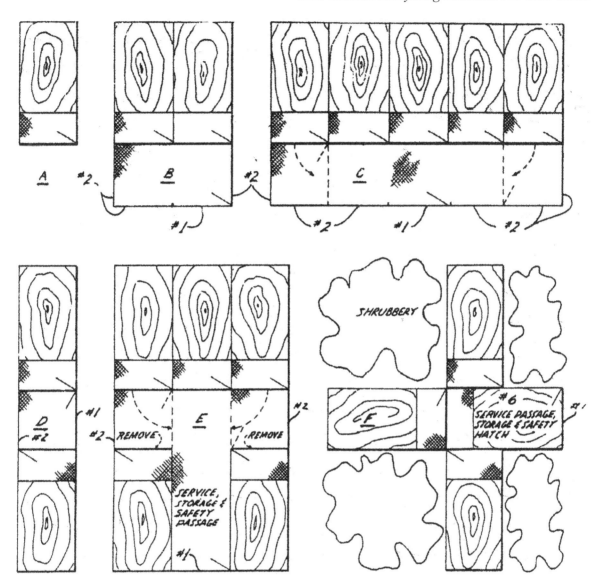

FIGURE 14 – LAYOUT ARRANGEMENTS POSSIBLE USING THE "STANDARD" FLIGHT AS THE BASIC UNIT. SINGLE-SIZE PANEL-FRAME AND SPACER TECHNIQUE OFFERS VARIATIONS OF AVIARY DESIGN LIMITED ONLY BY THE IMAGINATION OF THE BUILDER. ADDITIONAL LAYOUTS ARE IILLUSTRATED IN FIGURE 15. ALL LAYOUTS ARE SHOWN VIEWED FROM TOP:
A. SINGLE 4' X 8' X 6' HIGH FLIGHT. REFER TO FIGURES 7 & 8 FOR FRAMING DETAILS.
B. DOUBLE FLIGHT WITH ADDED 4' X 8' WIDE SAFE-PASSAGE. THE NUMBERS DENOTE PANELS USED TO ACHIEVE THIS ARRANGEMENT (SEE FIG. 7, PANEL REF. CODE NOS.)
C. EXTENSION OF LAYOUT B. THE ENTRANCE PANELS IN THE FIRST AND LAST FLIGHTS MAY BE SWUNG 90° TO EXTEND THEIR FLIGHT LENGTHS TO 12' (NOTE DASHED LINES).
D. DOUBLE FLIGHT WITH 4' X 4' SAFETY PASSAGE IN BETWEEN.
E. THOUGH SIMILAR TO LAYOUT "C" IN BOTH SQUARE FOOTAGE & MATERIAL COSTS, THIS LAYOUT HAS BUILT-IN ADVANTAGES. THE END FLIGHTS ARE EASILY CONVERTED TO EXTRA-LONG (20 FOOT) FLIGHTS AND THE ENTRANCE PASSAGE PROVIDES AMPLE SPACE FOR SERVICE & STORAGE.
F. THE UTMOST IN PRIVACY, WIND-PROTECTION, SOUND-PROOFING & CONDUCIVENESS TO BREEDING.

Construction Notes & Sketch Pad

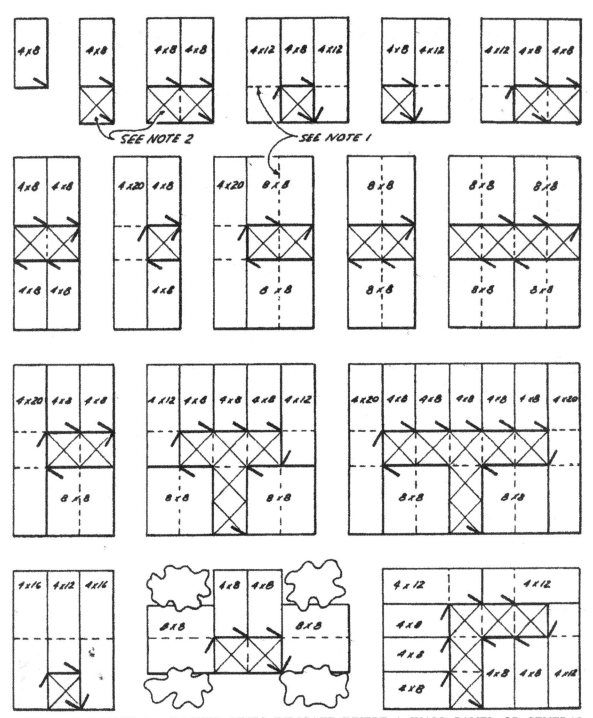

NOTE 1 – DASHED LINES INDICATE WHERE A WALL PANEL OR SEVERAL PANELS ARE DELETED IN ORDER TO EXTEND THE FLIGHT. THE AREAS, HOWEVER, SHOULD BE REINFORCED USING STANDARD PANEL "SHELLS" FOR THIS PURPOSE.

FIGURE 15 – ADDITIONAL AVIARY PLANS, UTILIZING STANDARD 4' X 8' FLIGHT AS THE BASIC UNIT OR "BUILDING BLOCK". SEE FIGURES 7 & 8 FOR PANEL FRAMING DETAILS.

<u>***Construction Notes & Sketch Pad***</u>

ALL WEATHER, INDOOR-OUTDOOR, Style 1

Figures 16, 17 and 18 describe an all-weather aviary which the builder will find is as utilitarian in the keeping of birds as it is secure against the elements of extreme climatic conditions.

The plan shown has six flights, although the structure is designed to tolerate more or fewer units without architectural upsets.

Each flight is 12 feet long by 3 feet wide, but is essentially a two room, indoor-outdoor affair in which the total length of the compartment is divided by a solid, all-weather wall which both isolates and insulates the interior flight portion from the exterior portion. Passage between both areas is provided by means of a small opening in the weather-wall which may be opened or closed by means of a bottom hinged, flap-type door. In extreme weather, birds in all of the occupied flights are quartered inside and all flap-doors are secured shut for protection. In milder situations, of course, the doors are left open to allow full flight exercising of the birds.

The interior portion of the aviary, again, is fully weather protected and, although not shown in the illustrations, may incorporate an appropriate heating unit for added security. Additionally conducive to long wintering is the fact that the interior flight portions contain larger volume or exercise space than their exterior counterparts. This is by way of the additional height provided by the raised and inclined roof, as shown in the illustrations. The raised roof design also provides the space required just under the eaves for the installation of a skylight window, essentially a 2 foot wide strip of translucent fiberglass fastened the full length of that space.

Included, also, in this plan is a service passageway which conveniently doubles as an escape trap and a storage area. Washtub and drain facilities, as well as electrical lighting and power outlets are also provided to make this, truly, a totally self-contained aviary.

The basic essentials required in constructing the aviary are described in Figure 17. Figure 18 includes, in more detail, the fabricating of the weather-wall and "flap" door, as well as the installation details of the fiberglass window. Additionally, information is given on how to initially lay out a foundation for the aviary itself.

All framing material, except where otherwise specified, is of the standard, so-called "2 X 2" boards with which, at this point, the builder should be fairly well acquainted.

The illustrated descriptions should pretty well cover all the information and details needed to proceed with actual construction, with the possible exception of roof-covering details and general finishing and painting instructions. These items, however, are again left to the discretion of the builder who, more often than not, prefers to exercise his own tastes in this area.

Construction Notes & Sketch Pad

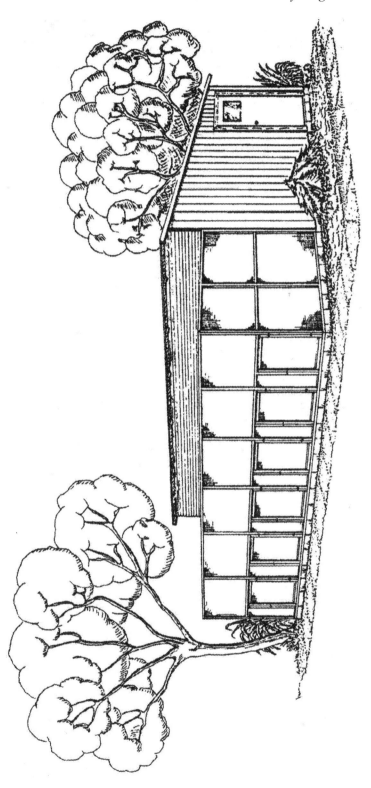

FIGURE 16 – ALL WEATHER, INDOOR-OUTDOOR AVIARY SUITABLE FOR EXTREMES IN CLIMATE. SPECIAL FEATURES INCLUDE INSIDE WINTERING QUARTERS, FULL 18 FOOT SKY-LIGHT, FOR DAYTIME INTERIOR LIGHTING, AND ELECTRICAL & PLUMBING FACILITIES.

Construction Notes & Sketch Pad

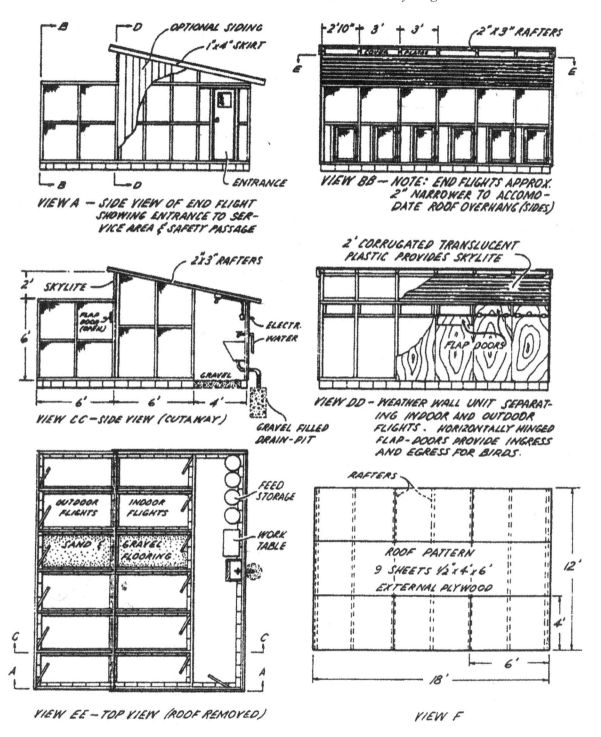

FIGURE 17 – STRUCTURAL DETAILS OF THE ALL-WEATHER, INDOOR-OUTDOOR AVIARY.

Construction Notes & Sketch Pad

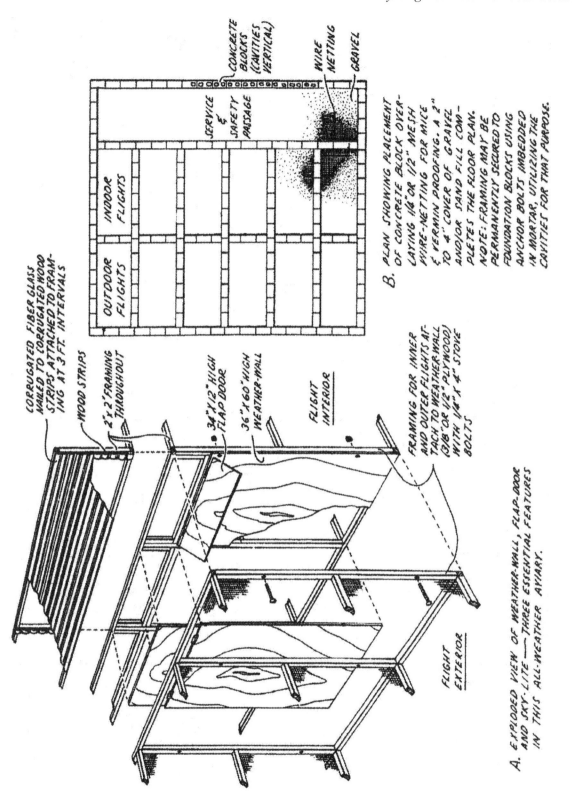

FIGURE 18 – DETAILS OF SKYLIGHT, FLAP-DOOR AND STRUCTURE FOUNDATION OF THE ALL-WEATHER AVIARY.

Construction Notes & Sketch Pad

ALL WEATHER, INDOOR-OUTDOOR, Style 2

Figures 19 and 20 illustrate somewhat of an extension to the preceding plan, and might very well be considered, depending on the ultimate interests and goals of the bird fancier, as the aviary of aviaries.

The basic plan and elevations only are given here, offering the builder much room for elaborating and applying minor (or major) deviations to suit his personal tastes, considering the generous size and potential costs represented here.

The structure, as shown, is a fairly large one, some 38 feet wide by 24 feet long and, at its' high point above the center passageway, approximately 12 feet in height. The full length of each flight in the aviary is 14 feet, 6 feet of which are enclosed within a weather-wall for winter quartering of the birds, and the remaining feet extending to the outside for use in milder climates. The width of each flight is 4 feet as described in this plan, but may easily be extended to 8 or more feet if desired, with ample support used to replace the removed flight walls.

In addition to the four-foot wide passageway which functions inside as an escape trap and service/storage area, there is, additionally, a three-foot wide, wire-enclosed passageway extending on both sides of the aviary to provide ample service and safety accommodations to the exterior portions of the flights.

The exterior wall surfaces of the main structure are covered with stucco texture and the roof is shingled or rolled to suit.

Interior lighting is provided by sun through fore and aft pairs of 4 foot square glass windows.

The total structure is built on construction blocks or poured concrete and uses 2" X 2"s for external flight framing and 2" X 3"s or standard "stud" material for the main structural framing.

When wire-netting all interior and exterior flight walls, care should be taken to cover any exposed wood pieces that remain, such as corner joints, with additional wire or metal sheet to prevent any possible damage by chewing birds.

METAL CONSTRUCTED AVIARIES

Figure 21 illustrates what can be done using metal pipe or angle-iron as the basic framing material in constructing individual flights or full aviaries. Metal piping, the diameter of which may vary from 1/2" to 1", depending on the ultimate flight size proposed, is somewhat tricky to use, since it requires very accurate dimensioning in cutting and threading pieces, as well as care in avoiding the "closed loop" problems involved in using this type material, as described in the illustration.

The angle iron method is much more simple to work with and, when completely fabricated, offers greater structural durability. The material costs, however, are greater.

Construction Notes & Sketch Pad

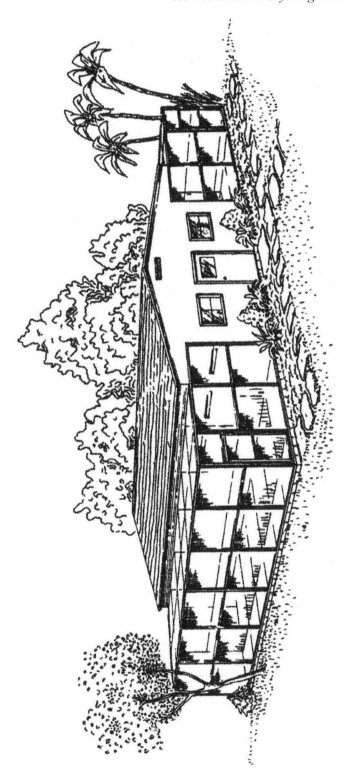

FIGURE 19 – DELUXE, ALL-WEATHER, INDOOR-OUTDOOR AVIARY FEATURING LARGE FLIGHTS, CENTRAL SERVICE & STORAGE PASSAGE AND TWO ADDITIONAL OUTSIDE PASSAGES LEADING TO INDIVIDUAL FLIGHTS. THE EXTERIOR MAIN STRUCTURE IS OF STUCCO, OR OPTIONAL SIDING OR BRICK AND LENDS ITSELF TO BEAUTIFUL LANDSCAPING.

Construction Notes & Sketch Pad

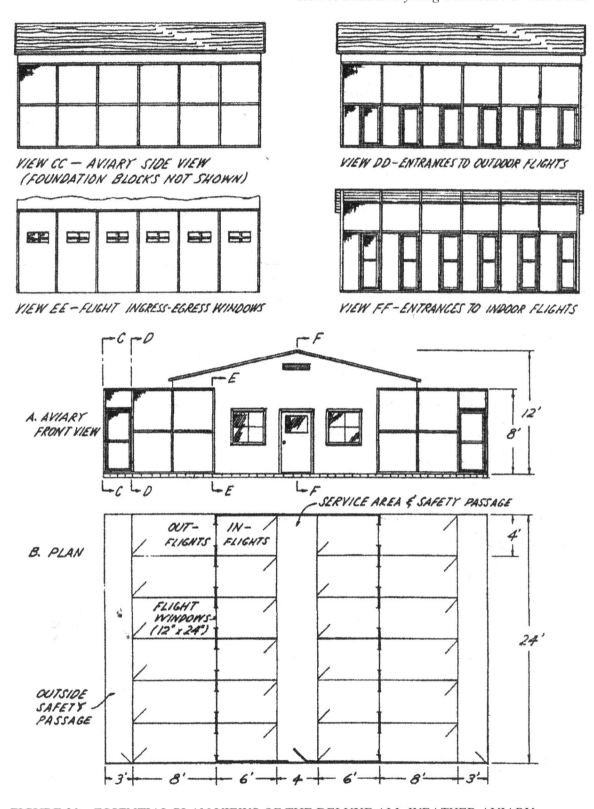

FIGURE 20 – ESSENTIAL PLAN VIEWS OF THE DELUXE ALL-WEATHER AVIARY

Construction Notes & Sketch Pad

A. PIPE-AND-FITTING SCHEME

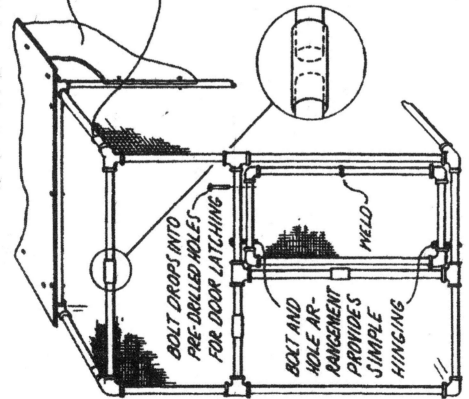

PLYWOOD OR ASBESTOS BOLTED TO PREDRILLED FRAMING PROVIDES SHELTERED AREA TO SUIT.

LARGE C-CLIPS (OR PIG RINGS) SECURE WIRE NETTING TO FRAMING.

FRAMING DESIGNS INCORPORATING THREADED PIPE & FITTINGS MUST INCLUDE UNION FITTINGS WHEREVER "CLOSED LOOPS" ARE DESIRED. HERE, A SIMPLE SLEEVE DEVICE SLIPS OVER THE SEVERED PIPE ENDS TO FORM AN EFFECTIVE UNION. SLEEVES MAY BE SECURED WITH SHEET METAL SCREWS. AN AL-TERNATE METHOD IS TO SPOT WELD THE SEVERED ENDS TO-GETHER (SHOWN ON DOOR AT LEFT).

BOLT DROPS INTO PRE-DRILLED HOLES FOR DOOR LATCHING

BOLT AND HOLE AR-RANGEMENT PROVIDES SIMPLE HINGING

WELD

FIGURE 21A

Construction Notes & Sketch Pad

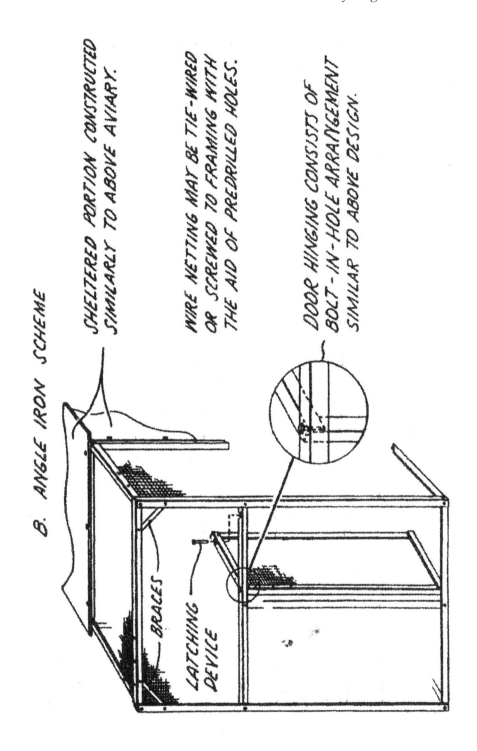

SHELTERED PORTION CONSTRUCTED SIMILARLY TO ABOVE AVIARY.

WIRE NETTING MAY BE TIE-WIRED OR SCREWED TO FRAMING WITH THE AID OF PREDRILLED HOLES.

DOOR HINGING CONSISTS OF BOLT-IN-HOLE ARRANGEMENT SIMILAR TO ABOVE DESIGN.

B. ANGLE IRON SCHEME

BRACES

LATCHING DEVICE

FIGURE 21B – TYPICAL CONSTRUCTION SCHEMES FOR METAL-FRAMED AVIARIES. PHYSICAL DIMENSIONS ARE OPTIONAL, THOUGH MORE DIFFICULT TO CONSTRUCT. METAL HOUSINGS HAVE AN ELEMENT OF STOUTNESS & ENDURANCE UNSURPASSED AMONG AVIARY TYPES.

Construction Notes & Sketch Pad

NEST BOXES

Figures 22 through 28 describe a generous assortment of nest boxes which are suitable for a variety of bird sizes from the tiny Finches to the immense Macaw.

Ample material callouts and dimensioning information is given, as well as assembly details provided, so that the hobbiest should be able to put together any one or a number of these projects with little or no difficulty.

A word of instruction might be appropriate here concerning the model suggested in Figure 23 and any other nest box, for that matter, which is intended for housing birds which do not normally use nesting materials to help contain their eggs. As shown in the figure, the base of this nest box incorporates a cavity or "concave" which is necessary for both collecting and holding the eggs in incubating position until they are hatched. There are any number of ways of achieving this concaved cut-out. The simplest is by using a half-moon shaped metal drill bit made for this purpose and which attaches to a standard drill press and literally bores out a hole into the shape of a concave. This tool is not readily available, however, and is usually custom machine-made, in fact, for those craftsmen who intend to commercially produce these type boxes on large orders.

The hobbiest who owns a circular radial-saw possesses the next best tool that is ideal for the problem. When properly set up, a concave may be formed simply by centering the base wood-piece on the saw table directly under the radius of the spinning blade, and lowering the blade slowly into the work as the piece is carefully rotated on its' vertical axis while it is held tightly to the table. The desired concave is achieved when the saw blade penetrates 1/4 to 1/2 inch into the wood. Needless to say, extreme caution must be taken in using power equipment in this manner, and a special holding jig or fixture for holding and manipulating the wood piece as it is being cut is highly recommended.

Another method of achieving a fairly good concave in wood is to apply a torch flame to the center portion of the wood piece and literally "burn" out a cavity. When the desired depth has been fairly well "charcoaled" and scraped away with a wire brush or coarse sandpaper, the finished cavity will provide a very satisfactory egg collector. Where the availability of the above type working tools is limited, a satisfactory cavity may be formed in wood simply by using the old tried and proven, though laborious, hammer and chisel method!

Indeed, a number of clever methods have been witnessed by the author during years as a bird-keeper; some methods had appropriate merit (and are mentioned above), but some he has personally judged as totally impractical, insofar as expense and labor are concerned. There are preformed, plastic mold inserts which are commercially sold, there are soft, pliable materials which can be "pounded" into shape, there are special bird compatible clay substances which may be carved and hardened into shape, etc., etc. In any case, however, for sake of immediate availability and utility, the author recommends the methods described above.

___Construction Notes & Sketch Pad___

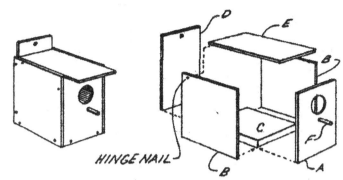

MATERIAL LIST

A. FRONT - ⅜" x 4½" x 5½" H.
B. SIDE (2)- ⅜" x 5¼" x 5⅝" H.
C. BASE - 1" x 4⅝" x 4½"
D. BACK - ⅜" x 4½" x 7" H.
E. TOP - ⅜" x 4½" W. x 7" L.
F. PERCH - ¼" x 2" LONG
NAILS - 1" CEMENT COATED
NOTE: LOCATE ENTRANCE HOLE
CENTER 3¼" FROM BOTTOM
& PERCH 2" FROM BOTTOM.

STANDARD "FLIP-TOP" BOX

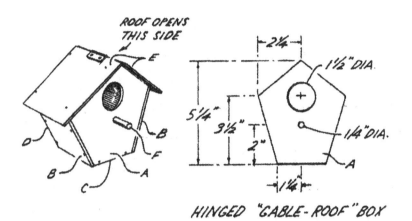

MATERIAL LIST

A. FRONT - DIM. SHOWN
B. SIDE (2) - ½" x 5" x 3⅝" H.
C. BASE - 1" x 2½" x 4¼" D.
D. BACK - SAME DIM. AS "A"
E. TOP (2) - ½" x 6" x 4" H.
F. PERCH - ¼" x 2" LONG
NAILS - 1" CEMENT COATED
HINGE - STD. 1" x 2" CABINET
NOTES - ROOF OVERHANGS AT
FRONT AND SIDES ONLY.
DRILL ¼" HANG-HOLE IN BACK.

HINGED "GABLE-ROOF" BOX

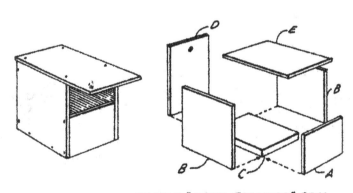

MATERIAL LIST

A. FRONT ⅜" x 5" x 3" H.
B. SIDE (2) ⅜" x 5¾" x 5" H.
C. BASE 1" x 5" x 5"
D. BACK ⅜" x 5" x 5" H.
E. TOP ⅜" x 6" W. x 7" L.
NAILS - 1" CEMENT COATED
NOTES: TOP IS PERMANENT-
LY ATTACHED (NO HINGING RE-
QUIRED) AND OVERHANGS AT
SIDES. NO PERCH IS REQUIRED.

SIMPLE "OPEN-FRONTED" BOX

FIGURE 22 – VARIATIONS OF NEST-BOXES SUITABLE FOR FINCHES & SMALL BILLED BIRDS.

Construction Notes & Sketch Pad

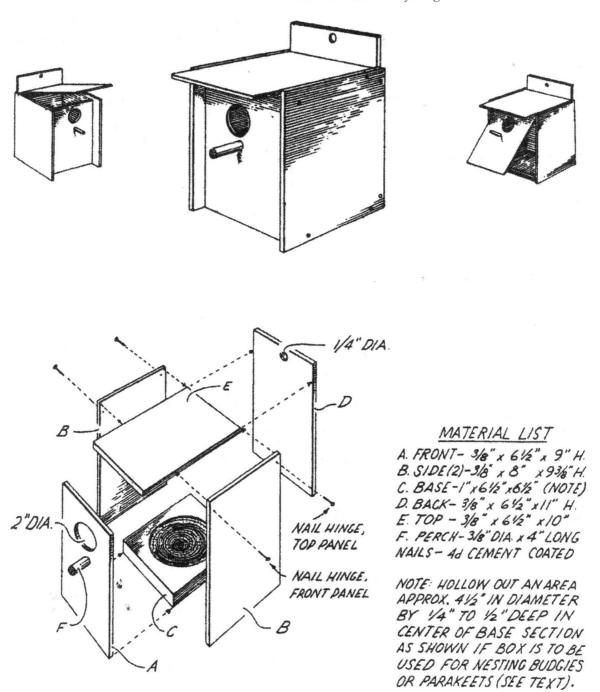

MATERIAL LIST
A. FRONT- 3/8" x 6½" x 9" H.
B. SIDE(2)-3/8" x 8" x 9⅜" H.
C. BASE-1" x 6½" x 6½" (NOTE)
D. BACK- 3/8" x 6½" x11" H.
E. TOP - 3/8" x 6½" x 10"
F. PERCH- 3/8" DIA. x 4" LONG
NAILS - 4d CEMENT COATED

NOTE: HOLLOW OUT AN AREA
APPROX. 4½" IN DIAMETER
BY ¼" TO ½" DEEP IN
CENTER OF BASE SECTION
AS SHOWN IF BOX IS TO BE
USED FOR NESTING BUDGIES
OR PARAKEETS (SEE TEXT).

FIGURE 23 – NEST BOX SUITABLE FOR BUDGIES, LINEONATED PARAKEETS, LOVEBIRDS AND SIMILAR-SIZED BIRDS. ALTHOUGH 3/8" PLYWOOD IS SUGGESTED FOR PANEL THICKNESS, ½" TO ¾" THICK MATERIAL MAY BE USED FOR IMPROVED DURABILITY AND INSULATION. (Locate center of 2" diameter hole 2" from top of front and locate center of perch 4" from top.)

Construction Notes & Sketch Pad

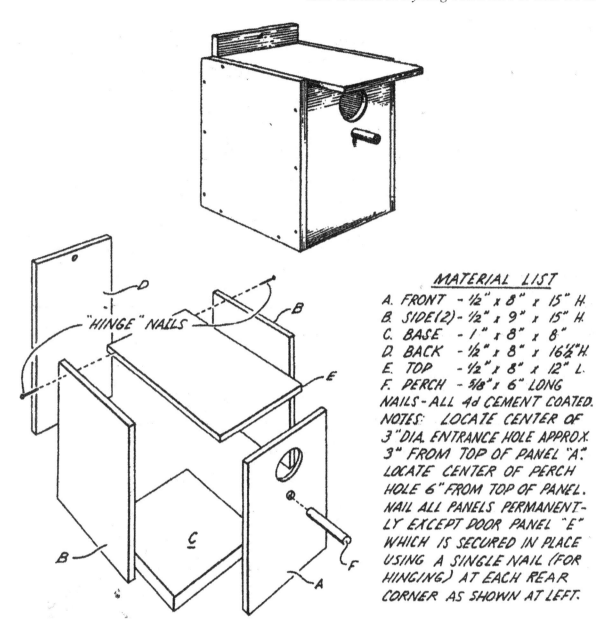

MATERIAL LIST

A. FRONT - ½" x 8" x 15" H.
B. SIDE(2) - ½" x 9" x 15" H.
C. BASE - 1" x 8" x 8"
D. BACK - ½" x 8" x 16½" H.
E. TOP - ½" x 8" x 12" L.
F. PERCH - 5/8" x 6" LONG
NAILS - ALL 4d CEMENT COATED.
NOTES: LOCATE CENTER OF
3" DIA. ENTRANCE HOLE APPROX.
3" FROM TOP OF PANEL "A".
LOCATE CENTER OF PERCH
HOLE 6" FROM TOP OF PANEL.
NAIL ALL PANELS PERMANENT-
LY EXCEPT DOOR PANEL "E"
WHICH IS SECURED IN PLACE
USING A SINGLE NAIL (FOR
HINGING) AT EACH REAR
CORNER AS SHOWN AT LEFT.

FIGURE 24 – NEST BOX SUITABLE FOR COCKATIELS, MOST OF THE CONURES AND BIRDS OF SIMILAR SIZE. MODIFICATIONS MAY CONSIST OF HOLLOWING OUT OF THE NEST-BOTTOM FOR THOSE BIRDS WHICH USE NO NESTING MATERIALS TO CONTAIN THEIR EGGS, FOR IMPROVED INCUBATION, THE ADDING OF ONE OF THE EASY-TO-MAKE MOISTURIZING DEVICES DESCRIBED IN FIGURES 29&30

Construction Notes & Sketch Pad

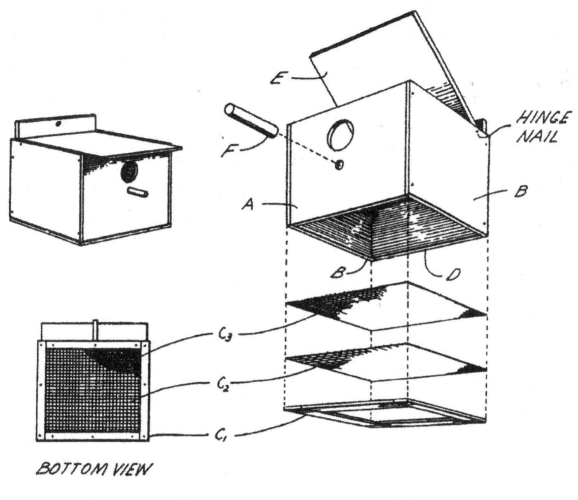

BOTTOM VIEW

MATERIAL LIST

A. FRONT - 3/4" x 12" x 11¼" HIGH
B. SIDE (2) - 3/4" x 10" x 12" HIGH
C₁. BASE FRAME - FOUR 1" STRIPS OF
   3/8" PLYWOOD. CUT TWO STRIPS
   10" LONG AND TWO 11½" LONG.
C₂. ¼" MESH SCREEN, 10" x 13½"
C₃. ⅛" MESH SCREEN, 10" x 13½"
D. BACK - 3/4" x 12" x 14" HIGH
E. TOP - 3/4" x 12" x 12" LONG
F. PERCH - 5/8" DIA. x 6" LONG
NAILS - 6d CEMENT COATED

NOTES

USE 6d CEMENT COATED NAILS
FOR HINGING TOP PANEL TO
SIDES AS SHOWN.
COAT INSIDE OF BOX, BOTTOM
EDGES AND BASE FRAME (C₁)
WITH NON-TOXIC PAINT OR
SEALANT BEFORE ASSEMBLING.
AFTER ASSEMBLY, COVER BOT-
TOM OF BOX WITH LAYER OF
PEA-SIZED CHARCOALS.

FIGURE 25 – NEST BOX FOR LORRIES AND LORIKEETS. THE SPECIAL BOTTOM OF WIRE-MESH AND ABSORBENT CHARCOAL-FILL PROVIDES A SIMPLE METHOD OF DEALING WITH THE HIGHLY LIQUID NATURE OF THE DROPPINGS OF THESE BIRDS. (Locate center of 3" diameter hole 3" from top of front and locate center of perch 6" from top.)

<u>*Construction Notes & Sketch Pad*</u>

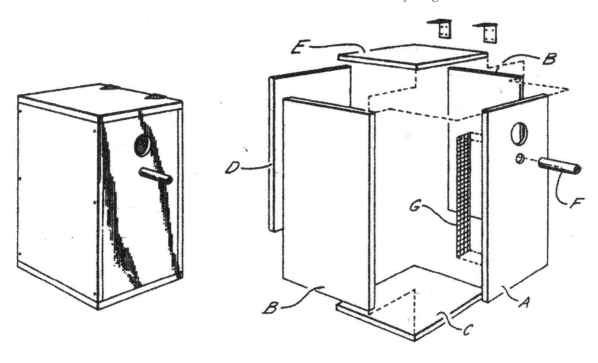

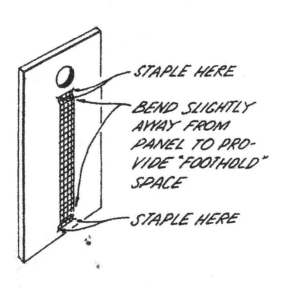

STAPLE HERE

BEND SLIGHTLY
AWAY FROM
PANEL TO PRO-
VIDE "FOOTHOLD"
SPACE

STAPLE HERE

MATERIAL LIST

A. FRONT - ¾" x 15" x 30" HIGH
B. SIDE (2) - ¾" x 13½" x 30" HIGH
C. BASE - ¾" x 15" x 15" SQ.
D. BACK - ¾" x 15" x 30" HIGH
E. TOP - ¾" x 15" x 15" SQ.
F. PERCH - ¾" x 6" LONG
G. WIRE LADDER - ½" TO 1" WIRE-
   MESH, 3" WIDE BY 20" LONG.
   HINGES (2) - 1" x 3" STRAP

NOTES

LOCATE CENTER OF 3½" DIA.
ENTRANCE HOLE 6" FROM TOP OF
PANEL "A". LOCATE CENTER OF
PERCH 10" FROM TOP OF PANEL
ALL NAILS ARE 6d SIZE.

FIGURE 26 – NEST BOX FOR LARGER PARAKEETS, RING-NECKS AND ROSELLAS. THE WIRE LADDER PROVIDES A CONVENIENT STAIRWAY FOR THE YOUNG BIRDS WHICH COULD POSSIBLE BECOME TRAPPED & CONFINED IN THEIR NEST BEYOND THE FLEDGLING STAGE.

Construction Notes & Sketch Pad

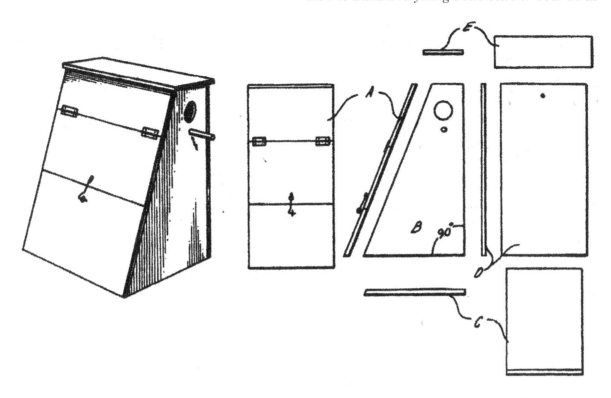

NOTES

PROVIDE WIRE LADDER LEAD-
ING FROM ENTRANCE HOLE
TO BOTTOM OF BOX, SIMILAR
TO PREVIOUS DESIGN. LOCATE
CENTER OF 3½" DIA. ENTRANCE
HOLE APPROX. 7" FROM TOP
OF EITHER ONE OF SIDE—
PANELS "B". LOCATE CENTER
OF 3/4" DIA. PERCH HOLE
APPROX. 11". FROM TOP OF
PANEL.

MATERIAL LIST

A. FRONT — 3/4" x 12" x 25½" HIGH.
DIVIDE INTO THREE EQUAL
PIECES USING CENTER PIECE
AS ACCESS DOOR. NOTE HINGING.
B. SIDE (2) 3/4" x 12" (AT BASE) x 24"
HIGH x 3½" (AT TOP).
C. BASE — 3/4" x 12" x 10½". AFTER
CUTTING TO SIZE, ANGLE FRONT
EDGE TO ACCOMODATE PANEL "A".
D. BACK — 3/4" x 12" x 24" HIGH.
E. TOP — 3/4" x 4" x 13".
HINGES (2) — STD. 1" x 2" CABINET
TYPE. NAILS — 6d CEMENT COATED.

FIGURE 27 – ANOTHER DESIGN SUITABLE FOR NESTING THE LARGER PARAKEETS, RINGNECKS AND ROSELLAS. THOUGH MORE DIFFICULT TO CONSTRUCT, THE ANGLED DESIGN, WITH ITS ALMOST RESTRICTED ENTRANCE LEADING TO LARGER NESTING QUARTERS BELOW, SEEMS TO APPEAL MORE READILY TO THESE TYPE BIRDS.

<u>*Construction Notes & Sketch Pad*</u>

A. IDEALLY SUITED FOR THE AMAZONS AND COCKATOOS, THIS NEST BOX IS MADE FROM AN OLD WINE BARREL (30 GAL. TYPE) CUT IN TWO, HORIZONTALLY, AND LINED INTERNALLY WITH HEAVY DUTY WIRE MESH. THE 5" ENTRANCE HOLE IS METAL-LINED.

METAL TRASH CANS (OR COMMERCIAL OIL OR CHEMICAL DRUMS) ARE EQUALLY SUITED FOR NESTING THE ABOVE BIRDS AND PROVIDE A DURABILITY NOT FOUND IN WOOD. (NOT SUITED FOR EXTREMELY HOT CLIMATES)

B.

HINGED DOOR

20"   36"

20"

C. A SUITABLE NESTING BOX FOR MACAWS IS ILLUSTRATED AT LEFT AND MAY BE CONSTRUCTED OUT OF 3/4" PLYWOOD, LINED INTERNALLY WITH WIRE MESH OR SHEET-METAL, AND PROVIDED WITH A METAL-LINED ENTRANCE HOLE APPROX. 7" IN DIA.

THIS NESTING BOX, THO SOMEWHAT DIFFICULT TO CONSTRUCT, HAS A UNIQUE DESIGN WHICH MORE NEARLY APPROXIMATES NATURAL NESTS FOUND IN THE WILD. THE DIMENSIONS SHOWN CAN BE MODIFIED TO ACCOMODATE MOST INTERMEDIATE TO LARGE BIRDS. 3/4" PLYWOOD IS USED THROUGHOUT AND A LADDER IS ENCLOSED FOR CLIMBING PURPOSES.

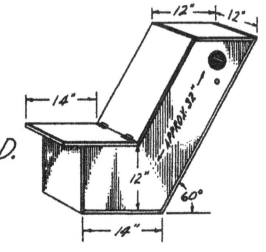

D.

12"   12"

14"

APPROX 32"

12"

60°

14"

FIGURE 28 – NEST BOX IDEAS FOR THE LARGER-SIZED BIRDS.

Construction Notes & Sketch Pad

MISCELLANEOUS EQUIPMENT

The illustrations and details on the next pages contain the rest of the necessary equipment you could require for the safety and health of your birds.

MOISTURIZING DEVICES

Figures 29 and 30 illustrate two inexpensive methods of insuring that the environment surrounding maturing eggs in a nest box remains humid and, therefore, more conducive to successful, live hatchings.

FEEDING EQUIPMENT

Figures 31, 32 and 33 suggest ideas for constructing and implementing feeding apparatus which is relatively inexpensive to make, although usually very costly to purchase on the market, particularly where large inventories of this equipment is required to supply a full-sized aviary. Several ideas are additionally suggested in **Figure 33** on how the aviculturalist may cope with persistently pesky and damaging mice and similar vermin.

HOSPITAL QUARTERS

Figure 34 describes a simple, inexpensive though efficient hospital cage which, when equipped with open feed dishes, medicated water for drinking, and standard thermometer, will provide the remaining essential ingredients of warm, humid fresh air required to assist the ailing bird toward recovery. The box may be used as a drying cage as well, by merely removing its evaporation unit (water pan) located under the floor.

The hospital quarters also have a possible temporary use as an inexpensive incubator for eggs if the need should arise and an incubator is not available. By adding a dimmer switch to the light bulb a fairly even temperature can be regulated in an emergency. This is definitely not as reliable as a commercial climate-controlled incubator, and not advised for any long term use or regular breeding program.

SHIPPING CONTAINER

Figure 35 illustrates and details a shipping container of a popular type used for transporting birds, particularly by air freight. This is a basic design which is easily modified to accept birds in a variety of sizes.

CARRYING CASE

Figure 36 describes a carrying case, also of a somewhat standard design, used in aviculture for the transporting of birds on a more local basis. For extended travel, a cloth or canvas cover can be fabricated which will provide the occupants with any necessary protection against the elements. This case is also easily modified to accept larger bird quantities or sizes.

<u>Construction Notes & Sketch Pad</u>

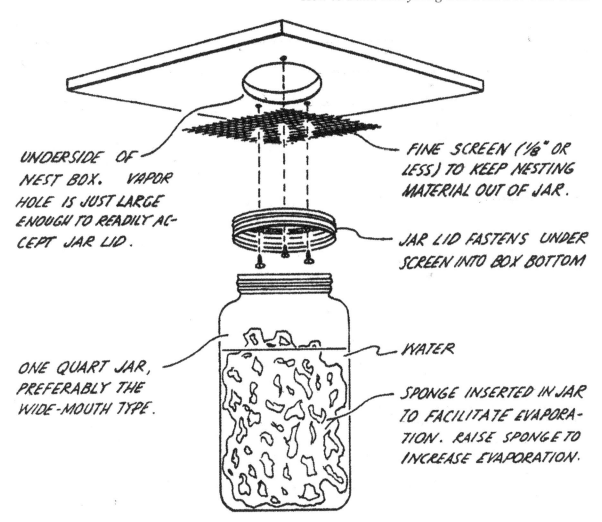

UNDERSIDE OF NEST BOX. VAPOR HOLE IS JUST LARGE ENOUGH TO READILY ACCEPT JAR LID.

FINE SCREEN (1/8" OR LESS) TO KEEP NESTING MATERIAL OUT OF JAR.

JAR LID FASTENS UNDER SCREEN INTO BOX BOTTOM

WATER

ONE QUART JAR, PREFERABLY THE WIDE-MOUTH TYPE.

SPONGE INSERTED IN JAR TO FACILITATE EVAPORATION. RAISE SPONGE TO INCREASE EVAPORATION.

FIGURE 29 – NEST BOX MOISTURIZER. A SIMPLE VAPORIZING DEVICE CONSISTING OF A QUART JAR, JAR LID, SPONGE, WIRE SCREEN TRAP AND MOUNTING SCREWS. PROPERLY FASTENED TO THE UNDERSIDE OF A NEST BOX IN WHICH A THRU-HOLE HAS BEEN DRILLED FOR PROPER VAPOR PASSAGE, THE ASSEMBLED UNIT WILL APTLY ASSIST MOST PSITTACINES IN PROVIDING THE ESSENTIAL HUMIDITY FOR MORE SUCCESSFUL EGG HATCHINGS. A VARIATION TO THE SINGLE LARGE VAPOR-HOLE MAY BE A SERIES MAY BE A SERIES OF SMALLER (1/4") HOLE DRILLED WITHIN A TOTAL CIRCUMFERENCE MARKED OFF WHICH IS LESS THAN THE CIRCUMFERENCE OF THE JAR LID. THIS IN COMBINATION WITH AN ADDITIONAL FINE SCREEN TRAP FASTENED ON THE INSIDE BOTTOM OF THE NEST BOX WILL FURTHER PREVENT NESTING MATERIAL FROM ENTERING THE WATER JAR.

Construction Notes & Sketch Pad

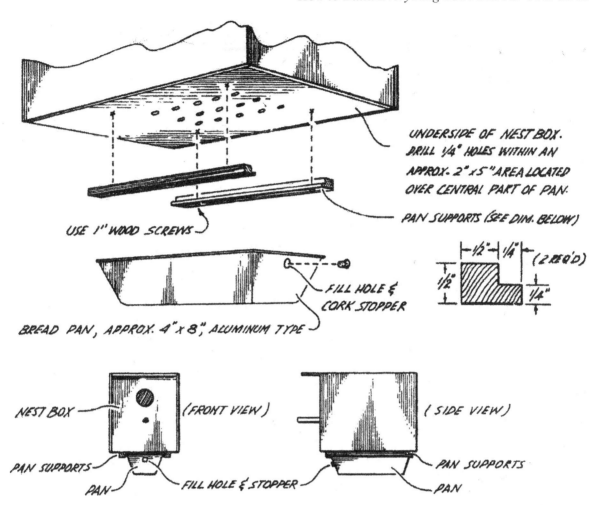

UNDERSIDE OF NEST BOX.
DRILL 1/4" HOLES WITHIN AN
APPROX. 2" x 5" AREA LOCATED
OVER CENTRAL PART OF PAN.

PAN SUPPORTS (SEE DIM. BELOW)

(2 REQ'D)

USE 1" WOOD SCREWS

FILL HOLE &
CORK STOPPER

BREAD PAN, APPROX. 4" x 8", ALUMINUM TYPE

NEST BOX

(FRONT VIEW)

(SIDE VIEW)

PAN SUPPORTS

PAN SUPPORTS

PAN

FILL HOLE & STOPPER

PAN

FIGURE 30 – NEST BOX MOISTURIZERS, PAN TYPE. ANOTHER VARIATION OF A MOISTURE GENERATING UNIT UTILIZING A STANDARD ALUMINUM TYPE BREAD PAN AS THE WATER CONTAINER INSTEAD OF THE QUART JAR AND SPONGE ARRANGEMENT DESCRIBED ON THE PREVIOUS PAGE. SPECIAL ADVANTAGES OF THE PAN SYSTEM ARE (1) GREATER WATER SURFACE EXPOSED AFFORDING GREATER EVAPORATION AND, HENCE, MORE PRONOUNCED HUMIDITY, AND (2) CONVENIENT REFILL PROVISION BY MEANS OF A CUT-OUT HOLE NEAR THE TOP OF THE PAN. SIZE OF BREAD PAN IS OPTIONAL, DEPENDING ON THE TYPE AND SIZE OF THE NEST BOX IT IS TO ACCOMMODATE, BUT, FOR BEST RESULTS, IT SHOULD BE AS LARGE AS POSSIBLE WITHOUT ACTUALLY OVERLAPPING THE UNDERSIDE EDGES OF THE NEST BOX WHEN ASSEMBLED. PAN SUPPORT LENGTHS ARE SIMILARLY OPTIONAL. FINE SCREEN FASTENED TO THE INSIDE BOTTOM OF BOX IS ALSO SUGGESTED.

<u>Construction Notes & Sketch Pad</u>

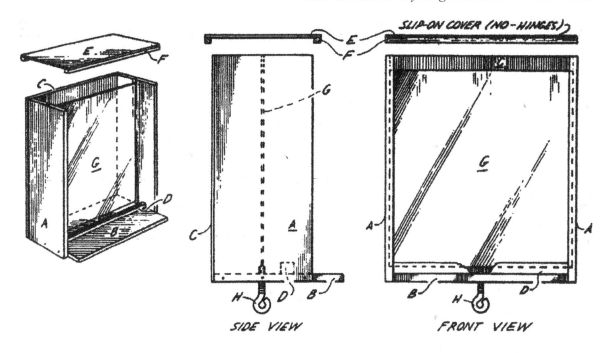

SIDE VIEW   FRONT VIEW

MATERIAL LIST

A. SIDES – 2 REQ'D – ½" PINE OR PLYWOOD CUT 6"
WIDE BY 14" HIGH. MARK A PENCIL LINE DOWN
THE MIDDLE OF EACH CUT PIECE, LEGNTHWISE, AND,
WITH A POWER SAW, CUT A KERF (SLOT) APPROX.
¼" DEEP BY ⅛" WIDE, THE FULL LENGTH OF EACH
BOARD. THE SLOTS ARE TO ACCOMODATE THE ⅛"
GLASS PLATE DURING FINAL ASSEMBLY.

B. BASE – 1 REQ'D – ½" PINE CUT 8" WIDE BY 11" LONG.
AFTER CUTTING, MEASURE OFF FROM THE BACK
EDGE 3 PENCIL LINES; ONE EACH AT 3", 4" AND
4¾". NEXT, LOCATE THE CENTER OF THE 3" MARKED
OFF LINE & DRILL A 3/16" HOLE TO ACCEPT THE EYE
BOLT USED FOR RAISING OR LOWERING THE GLASS
PLATE IN ADJUSTING FOR PROPER SEED FLOW. THE
REMAINING TWO MARKED OFF LINES ARE FOR LOCAT-
ING PLACEMENT OF SEED TRAP (D).

C. BACK PANEL – 1 REQ'D – ¼" PLYWOOD BY 12" W. BY 14" H.

D. SEED TRAP – 1 REQ'D – ¾" x ¾" x 11" LONG, PINE.

E. COVER – 1 REQ'D – ¼" PLYWOOD CUT 7½" W. BY 12" L.

F. COVER SUPPORTS – 2 REQ'D – ½" x ½" x 12 LONG, PINE.

G. GLASS PLATE – 1 REQ'D – ⅛" x 11½" W. x 12" H.

H. EYE BOLT, GLASS HEIGHT ADJUSTER – ¼" x 2" FULL THREAD.

MISC. – CEMENT COATED NAILS OR WOOD SCREWS TO SUIT.

FIGURE 31 – BIRD SEED FEEDER. CONSTRUCTED OF WOOD AND GLASS PLATE, THIS
ADJUSTABLE FEEDER WILL ACCOMMODATE SEED SIZES FROM LARGE SUNFLOWER
SEEDS ON DOWN AND KEEP USUALLY TROUBLESOME SEED WASTE TO A MINIMUM.

Construction Notes & Sketch Pad

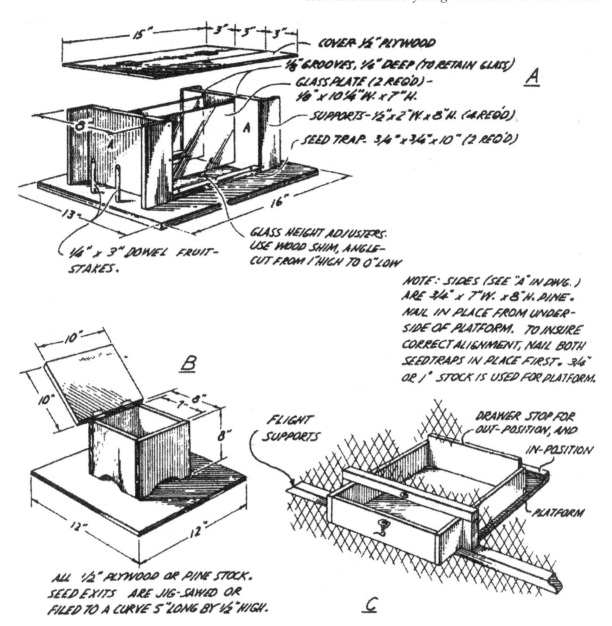

FIGURE 32 – MORE IDEAS FOR BIRD FEEDERS: FIGURE "A" ILLUSTRATES SOME DEGREE OF MODIFICATION FROM THE PRECEDING DESIGN AND IS ADAPTABLE FOR BOTH SEED AND MYNAH PELLETS. ADDITIONALLY, PROVISIONS ARE MADE AT EACH END FOR THE STAKING OF FRUIT HALVES, SUCH AS ORANGES, APPLES, ETC. ACCESS TO THE FEED CAN BE MADE FROM EITHER SIDE OR FROM ONE SIDE ONLY, DEPENDING UPON THE ADJUSTMENT (HEIGHT) OF THE GLASS PLATES. THE COVER NAILS DIRECTLY TO THE SIDES WITH THE EXCEPTION OF THE CENTER BOARD WHICH, INSTEAD, IS HINGED TO AN ADJACENT BOARD AND ACTS AS A SERVICE DOOR. FIGURE "B" IS A SIMPLY CONSTRUCTED SEED FEEDER WITH SEED EXITS ON ALL FOUR SIDES. FIGURE "C" IS A DRAWER-TYPE FEEDER WHICH CAN BE SERVICED FROM OUTSIDE. THE PLATFORM MAY BE WIRE SUSPENDED OR SUPPORT UNDERNEATH BY METAL BRACKETS OR GROUND POSTS. DIMENSIONS ARE OPTIONAL.

<u>*Construction Notes & Sketch Pad*</u>

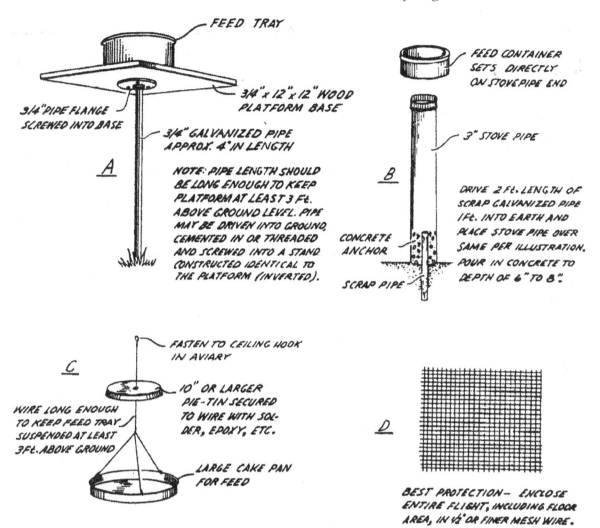

FIGURE 33 – MOUSE AND VERMIN-PROOFING FEED ACCOMMODATIONS. ALTHOUGH IT IS ALMOST IMPOSSIBLE TO INSURE TOTALLY AGAINST THESE PERSISTENT PESTS, ANY OF THE ABOVE SUGGESTIONS SHOULD FRUSTRATE AND DETER ALL BUT THE MOST ACROBATIC OF MICE FROM FOOD STEALING: FIGURE "A" CONSISTS OF A SIMPLE PIPE AND PLATFORM ARRANGEMENT WHICH DISCOURAGES ANY CLIMBING EFFORTS ATTEMPTED BY VERMIN. FIGURE "B" ILLUSTRATES THE SAME PRINCIPLE USING A LENGTH OF STOVE PIPE AS A PEDESTAL FOR THE FOOD TRAY. FIGURE "C" EMPLOYS A METHOD OF MICE-PROOFING COMMONLY USED ON SHIPS IN PORT, UTILIZING A METAL GUARD ON A TIE-DOWN ROPE (IN THIS CASE, A LENGTH OF WIRE SUSPENDED FROM THE FLIGHT ROOF) WHICH SERVES TO RESTRICT VERMIN TRAFFIC. FIGURE "D" DEPICTS THE ULTIMATE IN PROTECTION WHERE THE COSTS OF THE REQUIRED WIRE NETTING ARE NOT CONSIDERED PROHIBITIVE BY THE FANCIER.

Construction Notes & Sketch Pad

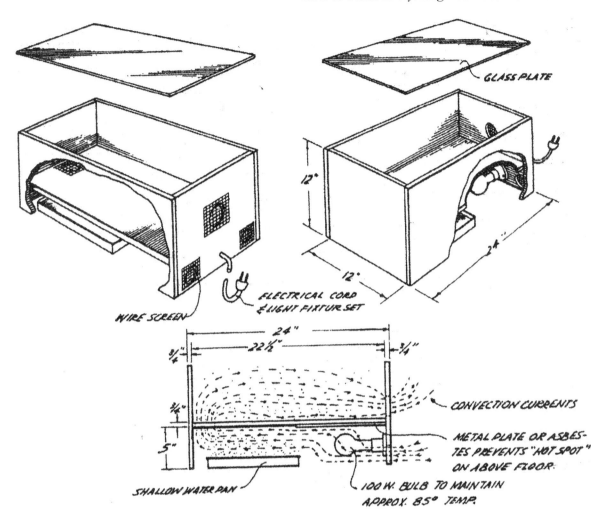

FIGURE 34 – HOSPITAL CAGE WHICH PROVIDES AN ESSENTIAL COMBINATION OF HIGH, EVEN TEMPERATURE WITH PLENTY OF FRESH, HUMID AIR FOR THE AILING BIRD, YET IS EASY TO CONSTRUCT. IN OPERATION, HEAT FROM A LAMP SOURCE PULLS IN OUTSIDE AIR, SETTING UP CONVECTION CURRENTS WHICH PICK UP MOISTURE AND MOVE TO PROPERLY VENTILATE THE UPPER, HOSPITAL COMPARTMENT. GLASS COVER KEEPS CLIMATE CONTAINED. ALL CONSTRUCTION IS OF ¾" PLYWOOD.

<u>*Construction Notes & Sketch Pad*</u>

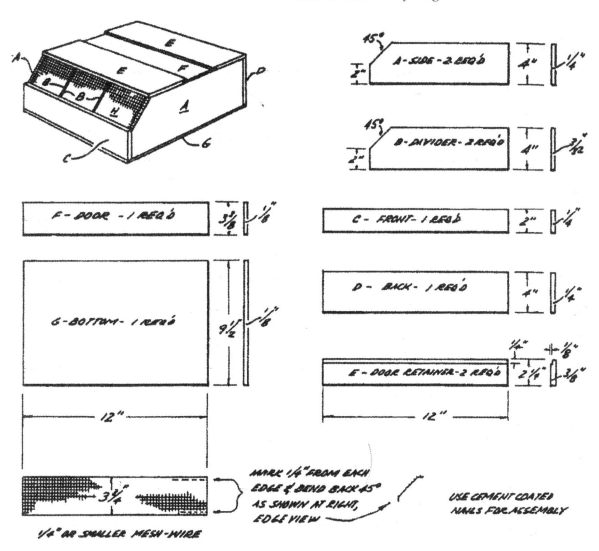

FIGURE 35 – A 3 COMPARTMENT SHIPPING CRATE FOR SHIPPING SMALL TO MEDIUM-SIZED BIRDS. SOFT, LIGHT WOODS, SUCH AS USED FOR FABRICATING APPLE-CRATES, ARE BEST SUITED FOR CONSTRUCTING THESE CAGES, SINCE SHIPPING COSTS ARE DIRECTLY RELATED TO WEIGHT FACTORS. THE WOOD THICKNESSES SHOULD APPROXIMATE AS CLOSELY AS POSSIBLE THOSE SPECIFIED IN THE ABOVE DIAGRAM. RECOMMENDED METHOD OF FASTENING THE SECTION DIVIDERS IS TO USE EPOXY GLUE ALONG ALL THE EDGES. THE BOX MAY BE MODIFIED FOR MORE THAN THREE COMPARTMENTS SIMPLY BY EXTENDING THE LENGTHS OF PIECES C, D, E, F, G, AND H AND INSERTING ADDITIONAL DIVIDERS. OR, WHEN NEEDED, ALL DIMENSIONS MAY BE INCREASED PROPORTIONATELY TO ACCOMMODATE LARGER BIRDS.

<u>Construction Notes & Sketch Pad</u>

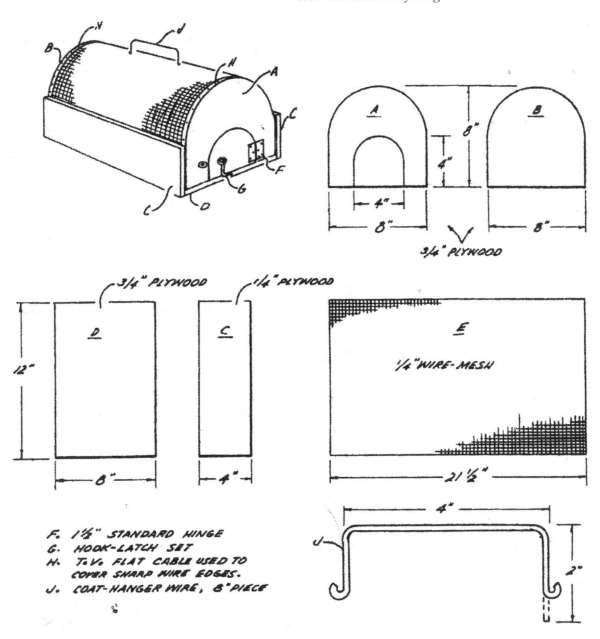

F. 1½" STANDARD HINGE
G. HOOK-LATCH SET
H. T.V. FLAT CABLE USED TO COVER SHARP WIRE EDGES.
J. COAT-HANGER WIRE, 8" PIECE

FIGURE 36 – CARRYING CASE – SUITABLE FOR MOST MEDIUM TO SMALL-SIZED BIRDS. PIECES "A" AND "B" BEGIN WITH TWO PIECES OF 8" SQUARE PLYWOOD OR PINE MARKED AT THE EXACT CENTER FROM WHICH A 4" RADIUS HALF CIRCLE IS DRAWN AND CUT ON A JIG SAW TO FORM THE TOP CURVE OF THE CASE. A DOOR IS CUT IN ONE OF THE TWO PIECES ("A") USING A 2" RADIUS MARKED FROM A POINT CENTERED 2" FROM THE BOTTOM AND REATTACHED USING A HINGE AS SHOWN. ASSEMBLE USING CEMENT COATED NAILS. THE ¼" MESH IS STAPLED OR NAILED TO ONE BOTTOM EDGE ("D") AND FINISHING ON OPPOSITE EDGE. COVER WIRE EDGES AS SHOWN WITH CABLE & INSTALL SIDE PIECES ("C").

<u>Construction Notes & Sketch Pad</u>

WIRING YOUR AVIARY

Figures 37 & 38 illustrates a very basic electrical wiring system that may be installed as shown or modified easily to suit any aviary type described in this manual. This particular system works nicely with the "Composite" aviary plan illustrated in **Figure 6**, servicing the flight and passage areas with two overhead lights, and the service/storage area with one light and one power receptacle or wall outlet. All three lights are wired to work on a single switch located at the entrance door, but additional on-off control of individual lights is possible simply by installing the type of porcelain light fixtures which have self-contained switches operated by means of pull strings. This arrangement is particularly advisable for those breeders who like keeping at least a single light burning during late hours for protective or other purposes. Indeed, some breeders insist that keeping a light on after dark actually enhances the survival rate of young birds, particularly during the short winter days, since the lighted quarters tend to discourage early retirement of the parent birds who are feeding their young.

Before beginning this, or any other wiring installation, find out if it is necessary in your locale to obtain a wiring permit first. It is not difficult to obtain one (if needed) provided you master the elementary wiring facts described here for our purposes, and that you acquaint yourself with some of the basic codes, or regulations, in your community. Your local Power Company can furnish this information if you describe to them what you intend to do.

Installation begins with attaching (usually nailing) all metal fixture boxes and junction boxes to appropriate supports, such as the roof and side panel framing (2 X 2's) of the aviary, wherever you feel they would be conveniently and strategically located for the most effective lighting and power service. Route all cabling, including the buried cable, as shown in the diagram, cutting to proper lengths and inserting the cable ends (at least 6" to 8" of cable) into the boxes through the proper "punch-out" holes, letting those ends dangle free for the moment. Fasten the total cable lengths at intervals along the framing members using cable straps or insulated staples made for this purpose.

Strip the insulation off all cable ends left protruding from the boxes, and interconnect all wiring indicated in the diagram, using twist-on solderless connectors. Make all necessary connections to the fixture terminals and install the fixtures on to their respective boxes.

After all wiring is checked carefully, and all fixtures installed properly, the power end of the buried cable may be connected to the appropriate circuit breaker or fuse at the service panel. If no "spare" breaker or fuse is available on the panel, you may have to purchase and install one yourself. There are usually spaces provided on the panel where one or more additional circuits may be installed for such cases like this. There is also usually a diagram on the panel cover giving installation and wiring instructions for adding new circuits (or this information can easily be obtained from any electrical supplier.) **Be sure all main power is off when working in this area!**

When all connections are completed and the power cable length is properly secured at both aviary and service panel ends, power may be turned on and all aviary fixtures checked for power and operation.

Construction Notes & Sketch Pad

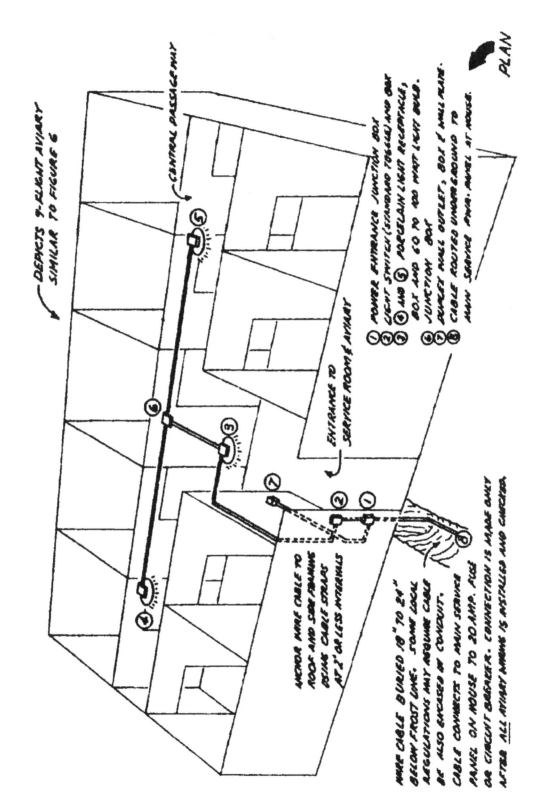

FIGURE 37 - BASIC ELECTRICAL SERVICE PLAN FOR AN AVIARY. CAN BE MODIFIED TO SUIT ANY AVIARY PLAN ONCE THE SIMPLE WIRING TECHNIQUES ARE MASTERED (see Figure 38).

<u>*Construction Notes & Sketch Pad*</u>

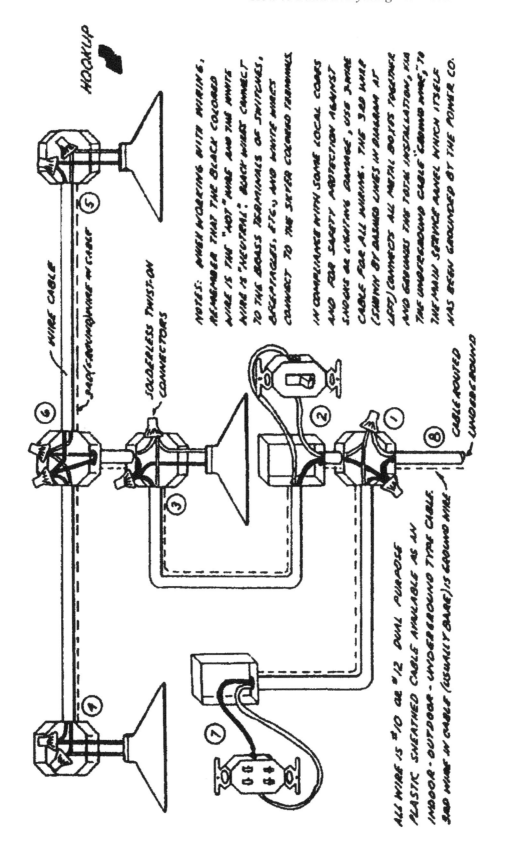

FIGURE 38 - BASIC WIRING TECHNIQUES FOR ELECTRICAL OUTLETS AND LIGHTS.

<u>*Construction Notes & Sketch Pad*</u>

ABOUT THE AUTHOR

Dominic LaRosa is a former breeder of exotic/caged birds with a BA in Education, and retired from more than thirty years in manufacturing engineering. At the time Dominic wrote *How to Build Everything You Need for Your Birds* in 1972, he was a free-lance technical illustrator, and a full-time bird breeder; designing and building his own aviaries. Drawing on his experience, he drafted the illustrations and wrote the book so others could find the information unavailable elsewhere. Obtaining a copyright and self-publishing in 1973, he has sold wholesale for thirty years and retail, on the internet, since 1999. He resides in Southern Oregon.

CPSIA information can be obtained
at www.ICGtesting.com
Printed in the USA
FSHW011033220120
66359FS

9 781403 346872